A

THE BIB

THE BOO

Tyndale House Publishers, Inc.
Carol Stream, Illinois

THE CRUCIFIXION WAS ONLY THE BEGINNING.

A.D.
THE BIBLE CONTINUES

THE BOOK OF ACTS

WITH NOTES AND INSIGHTS FROM

DR. DAVID JEREMIAH

New York Times Bestselling Author

Library of Congress Cataloging-in-Publication Data
Jeremiah, David, date.
   A.D. the book of Acts : the incredible story of the first followers of Jesus, according to the Bible / Dr. David Jeremiah.
      pages cm
   Includes bibliographical references.
   ISBN 978-1-4964-0718-4 (hc)
1. Church—Biblical teaching.   2. Bible. Acts—Criticism, interpretation, etc.   I. Title.
   BS2625.6.C5J47 2015
   226.6'06—dc23   2015000714

Printed in the United States of America

21	20	19	18	17	16	15
7	6	5	4	3	2	1

CONTENTS

INTRODUCTION

INTRODUCTION

"ALL HIS DISCIPLES deserted him and ran away" (Mark 14:50).

Such was the atmosphere in the garden of Gethsemane on the night Jesus was arrested. All his disciples ran for their lives, afraid of being arrested and put to death themselves. Peter's shame deepened just a couple of hours later, when three times he denied knowing Jesus.

Fast-forward fifty days, and these same disciples were risking their lives for Jesus. Something had obviously changed their minds—and their lives. In reality, there were two factors involved: the resurrection of Christ from the dead and the descent of the Holy Spirit at Pentecost. The Resurrection demonstrated God's power, and Pentecost delivered God's power. These two events transformed a fearful bunch of disciples into a forceful band of disciple makers who are responsible for the fact that you are reading these words today.

As far as we know, no one was writing down these events as they happened. No one was live-blogging, tweeting, or capturing the drama of those days on video. But in due course, a smart Gentile doctor was so impressed with the story of Jesus and the transformation of Jesus' followers that he, too, became a follower of Jesus.

A television commercial from years ago records a CEO saying, "I liked [the product] so much that I bought the company!" That could have been Luke in the first century; he was so impressed with the story of Jesus that he gave his life to it. With his education and abilities, he was an ideal candidate to commit the two-part story to writing: the inauguration of the church through Christ (the book of Luke) and the spread of the church through Christ's followers (the book of Acts). The prologues to both of Luke's books are evidence of the care he put into his research and writing (Luke 1:1-4; Acts 1:1-3).

As far as we know, Luke was not an eyewitness of the life of Christ—at least not as part of Christ's inner circle. For his book about the life of Christ, Luke "carefully investigated everything from the beginning" (Luke 1:3). For his book about the expansion of the church, however, he was doing real-time research. In Acts, Luke is able to give an up close account. On more than one occasion, he includes himself in the record of Paul's missionary travels and adventures (Acts 16:10-17; 20:5–21:18; 27:1–28:16).

In the Greco-Roman world, physicians such as Luke (Paul refers to Luke as "the beloved doctor" in Colossians 4:14) enjoyed high status as healers of the body and the mind. With such status came a commensurate level of wealth and prestige. Yet Luke sacrificed all that to join Paul in extending the Kingdom of God into Asia and Europe.

Luke and Paul would have been a good fit together in ministry. Luke's standing in the secular world was paralleled by Paul's reputation in the religious world. Paul enjoyed considerable esteem as a rising star among the Jewish leaders (Acts 22:3; Philippians 3:4-6). Yet Paul gave it all up, "counting it all as garbage" (Philippians 3:8) in order to devote his life to Christ. Perhaps Paul influenced Luke to do the same.

Paul and Luke were kindred spirits in their devotion to Christ and their passion for taking his gospel to the Gentiles. This was Paul's assignment from Christ (Acts 9:15-16; 22:21; 23:11; 26:15-18), and Luke joined his team as a supporter, scholar, doctor, and recorder. Luke's book of Acts is a multifaceted chronicle of Jesus Christ and what he did through his disciples, by the power of the Holy Spirit, to advance his Kingdom in the world.

The movement that started in Jerusalem expanded into Judea and Samaria and has continued "to the ends of the earth" (Acts 1:8). In fact, some say the words of Christ in Acts 1:8 are what Luke used as a general outline for his book.

THE PLAN OF ACTS

Just before his ascension into heaven, Christ told his disciples: "You will receive power when the Holy Spirit comes upon you. And you will be my witnesses, telling people about me everywhere—in Jerusalem, throughout Judea, in Samaria, and to the ends of the earth" (Acts 1:8).

Whether or not this was an intentional technique on Luke's part, we can outline the book of Acts based on these geographical cues:

- **Jerusalem** (Acts 1:1–8:3): the formation, rapid growth, persecution, and scattering of the believers in Jerusalem following Pentecost
- **Judea and Samaria** (Acts 8:4–12:25): the expansion of the church westward to the Mediterranean shores and north to Antioch of Syria
- **The ends of the earth** (Acts 13:1–28:31): the expansion of the church throughout Asia Minor, into Europe, and possibly as far west as Spain (Romans 15:24, 28)

Such an outline is sparse, to be sure. But it may provide a clue as to why Luke ends Acts where he does—six years before the death of the apostle Paul. At the end of Acts, Paul is under house arrest in Rome—his first Roman imprisonment—around A.D. 59–61. Luke concludes Acts with this description of Paul: "He welcomed all who visited him, boldly proclaiming the Kingdom of God and teaching about the Lord Jesus Christ. And no one tried to stop him" (Acts 28:30-31).

Paul's two-year imprisonment in Rome was a productive period. He wrote four letters (Ephesians, Philippians, Colossians, and Philemon) and received a stream of visitors and guests who came to hear the testimony of the famous Jewish scholar who had become a follower of Jesus (Acts 28:23-31; Philippians 4:22).

Besides possibly wanting to end his book on a positive note, why would Luke have put the final period where he did? After all, Paul was released from incarceration and then ministered another six years (this was the period when he might have made it as far west as Spain) before being rearrested, jailed, and martyred in Rome (2 Timothy 4:6-22). But Luke chose not to include this final chapter of Paul's life.

The reason is likely because Luke had made his point. He'd described the spread of the gospel from Jerusalem to Judea to Samaria and to Rome, the capital of the known Gentile world. That was Christ's command, and it had been fulfilled. Christ had told his disciples that they would "stand trial before governors and kings . . . [and] tell the rulers and other unbelievers about [him]" (Matthew 10:18). Jesus had also appointed Saul of Tarsus (the apostle Paul) to take the gospel "to the Gentiles and to kings" (Acts 9:15), and Paul had done that. Luke began his second book on a victorious note in Jerusalem and ended it on a victorious note in

Rome, which was an effective way to summarize what had happened—and what would continue to happen as the church took the gospel throughout the world.

Another way to outline the book of Acts is to center it on the book's key character: the apostle Paul. More than half of the book of Acts (chapters 13–28) chronicles Paul's missionary activity. Chapters 1–12 can be read as a prologue to Paul's work, as these chapters identify him as the leading persecutor of the church, describe his conversion to Christ, and record his pre-missionary activities.

- **Prologue** (Acts 1–12): The church is born; believers are persecuted and scattered; Saul of Tarsus, the Christians' chief persecutor, is converted; Paul is gradually accepted by the church.
- **Paul's first missionary journey and the council at Jerusalem** (Acts 13–15:35): Paul preaches to the Gentiles in Cyprus, Turkey, and Syria, taking Barnabas and John Mark with him; the council at Jerusalem declares that Gentiles who come to Christ do not need to be circumcised.
- **Paul's second missionary journey** (Acts 15:36–18:22): Paul and Silas strengthen churches in Syria; Paul travels throughout Greece, preaching and encouraging new believers (such as Lydia, Priscilla, and Aquila).
- **Paul's third missionary journey** (Acts 18:23–21:16): Paul ministers in Ephesus

(in modern-day Turkey) before returning
to Jerusalem, where he is arrested.
- **Paul's fourth "missionary journey"** (Acts
21:17–28:10): This is not a planned
missionary journey; it comes as a result of
Paul's arrest in Jerusalem and his appeal to
make his case to Caesar in Rome.
- **Epilogue** (Acts 28:11-31): Paul is incarcerated
in Rome.

Outlining the book this way affirms what
American poet and philosopher Ralph Waldo
Emerson believed: that all history is biography. In
addition to recounting key events in Paul's life, Acts
is filled with descriptions of other people we can
learn from.

Another lesson we can glean from this overview
of Paul's conversion and ministry is that God always
has a plan. Paul wouldn't have mapped out his life
this way—particularly not being struck with blind-
ness for several days or being imprisoned for several
years—but it's clear in retrospect that God's plan
was sovereign even in these apparent setbacks.

How would you outline your own life?
Thematically, geographically, or chronologically?
Based on high points and low points? It doesn't
really matter, because all are relevant. God is always
at work in our circumstances with "a plan to fulfill
his own good pleasure" (Ephesians 1:9).

The path of the gospel from Jerusalem to Rome
and to "other places far beyond" (2 Corinthians
10:16) is not a straight line. There were, and will

continue to be, twists and turns, starts and stops, all along the way. But in the end, God's plan is always fulfilled: "We can make our plans, but the LORD determines our steps" (Proverbs 16:9).

The same is true of our lives. On the front, our lives look like a beautiful tapestry. But on the back, there are all kinds of knots and tie-offs and connections and repairs that make the front of the masterpiece possible. The book of Acts can look a bit "messy" at times, just like our lives do. But all of this is ultimately part of God's plan to build his church (Matthew 16:18) and conform us to the image of Christ (Romans 8:29), regardless of the difficulties involved (Romans 8:28).

The book of Acts reveals five ways God grew the church in the first century—and how he will continue to grow it until Christ returns. In addition to the plan of Acts, we will look at the people, places, providence, provision, and power in this book as principles for growing God's church.

PEOPLE IN ACTS

The two most prominent people in the New Testament are Jesus Christ and the apostle Paul. But there is something surprising about both of them: we might have passed either of them on the street or been introduced to them in a meeting without being impressed with their outward appearances. There is very little mentioned about their physical looks in Scripture, but what we do know is rather surprising.

The prophet Isaiah foretold this description of the coming Messiah: "There [would be] nothing beautiful or majestic about his appearance, nothing to attract us to him" (Isaiah 53:2). As for the apostle Paul, his critics said that "in person he is weak, and his speeches are worthless!" (2 Corinthians 10:10). Those characterizations confirm what we find in the book of Acts: God uses ordinary people, empowered by the Holy Spirit, to grow his church. The individuals he chooses may be attractive, eloquent, and learned . . . or not. As God told the prophet Samuel when he was choosing a king for Israel, "The LORD doesn't see things the way you see them. People judge by outward appearance, but the LORD looks at the heart" (1 Samuel 16:7).

Think of the variety of people Luke identifies in the book of Acts. There is no predictable pattern at all. There were unnamed women gathered in prayer, perhaps praying for the gift of the Holy Spirit to come (Acts 1:14). There was a repentant disciple named Peter, who had been forgiven and restored to ministry (Acts 2:14; 4:19-20; 5:3-29). Two disciples, Joseph and Matthias, were nominated to replace Judas Iscariot. Matthias was chosen, but we never hear of either again (Acts 1:23-26). These believers are like most of us—behind-the-scenes Christians living faithful lives, serving where needed, contributing to the Kingdom.

Among Jesus' followers were also scholars such as Paul and Luke. There were generous encouragers such as Barnabas (Acts 4:36-37). The book of Acts also mentions disabled and afflicted people whose needs were miraculously met and who were unashamed to praise God on the spot (Acts 3:6-10; 5:15). Seven men were given important administrative roles as deacons—all served, but only two receive additional coverage from Luke (Acts 6:5-6).

This book also includes people from a wide range of cultural backgrounds. There was an African official who returned to Ethiopia with the gospel (Acts 8:26-40) and a Roman centurion whose family and household gladly believed in Christ (Acts 10). The same was true for a Roman jailer in Philippi (Acts 16:33). Then there was Lydia, a businesswoman in Philippi, who started a church in her home (Acts 16:11-15). A married couple named Aquila and Priscilla encouraged Paul (Acts 18:2, 18), and a powerful Jewish-Christian orator named Apollos refuted the Jewish leaders' arguments (Acts 18:24-29). The list goes on and on.

Do you see yourself in that list? If not, keep reading and you will surely find yourself on the pages of Acts. You will see how God used—and still uses—people just like you to expand his Kingdom on earth.

PLACES IN ACTS

A significant portion of our lives are decided by a simple question: "Where?" While many places in our lives seem mundane and inconsequential—the grocery store, the gym, the doctor's office, the gas station—that's not the right way to view them. *Every* place in life is a location of consequence in God's sight. Acts 17:26 says, "From one man he made all the nations, that they should inhabit the whole earth; and he marked out their appointed times in history and the boundaries of their lands" (NIV). That definitely includes where we go and why God has directed our steps to those places.

It would be a mistake to view our lives as commonplace in God's sight compared to the lives of the believers in Acts. It might be tempting to assume that God sent the apostles to specific, important places while we're left to wander from place to place in our inconsequential lives. But nothing could be further from the truth!

The book of Acts offers only a bare-bones outline of where the apostles were instructed to go: they were to leave Jerusalem, go to Judea and Samaria, and then make their way to the rest of the world (Acts 1:8). Without taking anything away from the gravity of the command, this was a commonsense set of directions. Jerusalem was in Judea, and Samaria was right next to Judea. After that comes the rest of the world—"the ends of the earth" (Acts 1:8). When embarking on a daunting new venture, it makes sense to begin with your neighbors and then move on from there.

The apostles' task is the same one you and I have. We are just as "sent" as they were. The places we go are just as important as the places they went. Why? Because where they went, and where we go, is where Christ goes in this world. We don't just go to the grocery store to buy food; we go there as "Christ's ambassadors" (2 Corinthians 5:20) to accomplish whatever needs to be done for him: an act of kindness extended, a word of encouragement offered, a lesson taught, a testimony or witness shared—all in the name of Christ.

A number of years ago the book *In Search of Excellence* popularized the concept of "management by walking around." The idea encouraged corporate executives to leave their paneled offices and get onto the factory floors, where problems are solved, opportunities are uncovered, and lives are changed. If you read the book of Acts with an eye for place, you'll see that Paul and the other believers conducted their mission for Christ in a similar way: "mission by walking around."

They believed that they were sent, that Christ was with them, and that the Holy Spirit was guiding and empowering them. As a result, they also believed they would bear fruit. They looked for closed doors and open doors (Acts 16:6-10). They believed that there was a purpose for every person they met (Acts 16:11-15). And they took advantage of every opportunity. For example, when they were in jail in Philippi, they decided there must be a reason for it—a calling God had for them in that place. They were convinced that nothing was random. And they were right: God used their imprisonment to bring salvation to the Philippian jailer and his family (Acts 16:25-34).

The entire book of Acts is filled with stories like this one. The apostles believed they'd been placed where they were for a reason, and we should follow their example. Trust that your daily movements, in both significant and insignificant places, can be divine appointments. Be sensitive to every nuance of the Spirit, trusting him to use you to expand his Kingdom place by place.

Providence in Acts

Closely tied to the idea of place in Acts is the doctrine of God's providence—his overarching supervision and ordering of the affairs of the world to accomplish his perfect plans and purposes. As New Testament scholar D. A. Carson writes, providence is a mystery: "The mystery of providence defies our attempt to tame it by reason. I do not mean it is illogical; I mean that we do not know enough to be able to unpack it."[1]

And because providence is a mystery, what the great Reformer John Calvin said is also true: "There is nothing of which it is more difficult to convince men than that the providence of God governs this world." In the moment, it is often difficult to see the hand of God. But when faithful eyes exercise hindsight, it is much easier to see the hand of God in the midst of our affairs.

There are plenty of examples of God's providence in the book of Acts—events that seem unreasonable or illogical from a human perspective but serve as graphic illustrations of Romans 8:28-29—that God causes all things to work together for good in the lives of those he is conforming to the image of Christ. Although there are countless examples of God's providence throughout the book of Acts, here are a few that stand out.

- **Pentecost** (Acts 2:1-13): Christ told the apostles to go into all the world with the gospel. Shortly after Jesus gave this command, devout Jews—thousands of them!—from a multitude of nations gathered in Jerusalem for Pentecost, all speaking different languages. It would have taken years for the apostles to reach people from so many nations, but here they were providentially gathered right in the apostles' own city. Many of these people heard the gospel, believed it, and were baptized, and then they took the gospel back to their homelands. None of the apostles could have seen this coming. But they stepped into the flow of God's movement, and world missions was born in a day.

- **Persecution** (Acts 4–5): The apostles were beaten, berated, and jailed in the days following Pentecost. But this persecution gave them the opportunity to preach before the Sanhedrin (the ruling body of the Jews) several times (Acts 4:5-13; 5:27-31). The apostles never could have orchestrated such opportunities on their own.

- **Martyrdom** (Acts 7:54–8:2): Stephen was martyred in Jerusalem, and persecution broke out against Christians. As a result, "all the believers except the apostles were scattered through the regions of Judea and Samaria" (Acts 8:1). Did you catch that? They were sent to Judea and Samaria— exactly where Christ had told them to begin evangelizing (Acts 1:8). The apostles could have formed a committee to vote on the best mission strategy, but instead they went with what God was doing in their midst.

- **Arrest, jail, and shipwreck** (Acts 21–28): Jesus told Paul he would preach to Gentile kings, but he didn't specify how (Acts 9:15). Paul was arrested in Jerusalem, imprisoned in Caesarea for two years, and shipwrecked in the Mediterranean before he finally reached Rome. Would he have planned it that way? Probably not. But he didn't question what God was doing. He let events unfold according to God's timetable.

Don't make the mistake of thinking that God's providence only relates to "big" things—the movements of kings and nations. As the classic theologian A. A. Hodge writes, "special" (individual) providence is equally important: "To admit universal providence and deny special is nonsense. You might as well talk of a chain without any links."[2]

Are you willing to let God use the events in your life as links in his providential chain to extend his Kingdom on earth? Can you see those events the way he does and step into his flow with submission and thanksgiving?

PROVISION IN ACTS

The root word for *providence* is the same as the root for *provision*. Both words are based on a compound

Latin word: *pro* ("before") and *videre* ("to see"). In other words, to provide is "to foresee" or "to attend to."

When Paul was under house arrest in Rome (Acts 28:16-31), he was totally dependent on God to supply his needs. This was true during his entire ministry, of course, but it was especially the case when he was under arrest and couldn't work at his trade of making tents (Acts 18:3). One of the letters he wrote while he was incarcerated provides a clear example of how God provided for him. The church in Philippi had sent gifts to sustain Paul, and in his letter he thanked them profusely (Philippians 4:10-20). He promised them that, as they had supplied his needs, God would provide for them in return (Philippians 4:19).

The ideas of divine provision and providence are based on God's ability to foresee our needs. He knows the future; he knows what we *have* compared with what we will *need*. And he is prepared to meet those needs as we trust in him. The church in many parts of the world, the United States included, operates out of its abundance, not its poverty, as the first-century church did (2 Corinthians 8:1-2). But if we are going to model our faith and fruit after the first-century church, we will need to learn to trust God the way they did—not just for money, but for everything required to finish the task they started.

Power in Acts

The most important element needed to build the early church was God's power. In the same instructions—the same verse—where Jesus gave the apostles an assignment, he also gave them the resource they would need to carry out that assignment. They were to go into Judea, Samaria, and the rest of the world, but they weren't left powerless to fulfill this mission: "You will receive power when the Holy Spirit comes upon you" (Acts 1:8).

The implication is clear: we aren't to attempt to be witnesses for Christ apart from the presence and resulting power of the Holy Spirit. The connection immediately became obvious for the apostles. When the Holy Spirit fell upon them and they were given the gift of languages, they began bearing fruit. The formerly fearful and shamed disciple Peter stood up and preached in a manner that must have surprised the Galilean fisherman even more than it surprised everyone else. As a result of his preaching, three thousand souls were added to the church that day (Acts 2:41).

The power of God was working through the apostles in miraculous ways as God verified their roles and their authority in the church throughout the book of Acts (Acts 3:6-7; 4:30; 5:1-11, 12-16; 6:8; 8:6-7, 13; 9:32-35; 14:3; 15:12; 19:11-12; 20:9-12; 28:1-10). Those powers were given to the apostles for a specific purpose: to prove that they were God's ambassadors as the early church was birthed (2 Corinthians 12:12). The church today should not expect the wholesale duplication of that kind of power.

What we can expect is the power of the Holy Spirit in every realm of our lives. The Holy Spirit gives us the power to develop the character of Christ (Galatians 5:22-23), the power to minister as we have been gifted by the Spirit (1 Corinthians 12:8-11), the power to overcome obstacles we face (2 Corinthians 12:7-10), and the power to boldly and courageously defend the gospel against the attacks of the evil one (Ephesians 6:10-18).

I invite you to join the "huge crowd of witnesses" (Hebrews 12:1) who have gone before us by imitating their faith and obedience. God's plan for his church has already been established, and he is still at work in places around the world, acting through people who are directed by his providence, fueled by his provision, and empowered by his Spirit—until Jesus returns for his church.

God continues to write the book of Acts—but now he is writing through his people.

Dr. David Jeremiah
January 2015

PROLOGUE

PROLOGUE

THE LAST DAYS OF JESUS

LUKE 23:13–24:53

The Last Days of Jesus

Then Pilate called together the leading priests and other religious leaders, along with the people, and he announced his verdict. "You brought this man to me, accusing him of leading a revolt. I have examined him thoroughly on this point in your presence and find him innocent. Herod came to the same conclusion and sent him back to us. Nothing this man has done calls for the death penalty. So I will have him flogged, and then I will release him."

Then a mighty roar rose from the crowd, and with one voice they shouted, "Kill him, and release Barabbas to us!" (Barabbas was in prison for taking part in an insurrection in Jerusalem against the government, and for murder.) Pilate argued with them, because he wanted to release Jesus. But they kept shouting, "Crucify him! Crucify him!"

For the third time he demanded, "Why? What crime has he committed? I have found no reason to sentence him to death. So I will have him flogged, and then I will release him."

But the mob shouted louder and louder, demanding that Jesus be crucified, and their voices prevailed. So Pilate sentenced Jesus to die as they demanded. As they had requested, he released Barabbas, the man in prison for insurrection and murder. But he turned Jesus over to them to do as they wished.

THE CRUCIFIXION

As they led Jesus away, a man named Simon, who was from Cyrene, happened to be coming in from the countryside. The soldiers seized him and put the cross on him and made him carry it behind Jesus. A large crowd trailed behind, including many grief-stricken women. But Jesus turned and said to them, "Daughters of Jerusalem, don't weep for me, but weep for yourselves and for your children. For the days are coming when they will say, 'Fortunate indeed are the women who are childless, the wombs that have not borne a child and the breasts that have never nursed.' People will beg the mountains, 'Fall on us,' and plead with the hills, 'Bury us.' For if these things are done when the tree is green, what will happen when it is dry?"

Two others, both criminals, were led out to be executed with him. When they came to a place called The Skull, they nailed him to the cross. And the criminals were also crucified—one on his right and one on his left.

Jesus said, "Father, forgive them, for they don't know what they are doing." And the soldiers gambled for his clothes by throwing dice.

The crowd watched and the leaders scoffed. "He saved others," they said, "let him save himself if he is really God's Messiah, the Chosen One." The soldiers mocked him, too, by offering him a drink of sour wine. They called out to him, "If you are the King of the Jews, save yourself!" A sign was fastened above him with these words: "This is the King of the Jews."

One of the criminals hanging beside him scoffed, "So you're the Messiah, are you? Prove it by saving yourself—and us, too, while you're at it!"

But the other criminal protested, "Don't you fear God even when you have been sentenced to die? We deserve to die for our crimes, but this man hasn't done anything wrong." Then he said, "Jesus, remember me when you come into your Kingdom."

And Jesus replied, "I assure you, today you will be with me in paradise."

The Death of Jesus

By this time it was about noon, and darkness fell across the whole land until three o'clock. The light from the sun was gone. And suddenly, the curtain in the sanctuary of the Temple was torn down the middle. Then Jesus shouted, "Father, I entrust my spirit into your hands!" And with those words he breathed his last.

When the Roman officer overseeing the execution saw what had happened, he worshiped God and said, "Surely this man was innocent." And when all the crowd that came to see the crucifixion saw what had happened, they went home in deep sorrow. But Jesus' friends, including the women who had followed him from Galilee, stood at a distance watching.

THE BURIAL OF JESUS

Now there was a good and righteous man named Joseph. He was a member of the Jewish high council, but he had not agreed with the decision and actions of the other religious leaders. He was from the town of Arimathea in Judea, and he was waiting for the Kingdom of God to come. He went to Pilate and asked for Jesus' body. Then he took the body down from the cross and wrapped it in a long sheet of linen cloth and laid it in a new tomb that had been carved out of rock. This was done late on Friday afternoon, the day of preparation, as the Sabbath was about to begin.

As his body was taken away, the women from Galilee followed and saw the tomb where his body was placed. Then they went home and prepared spices and ointments to anoint his body. But by the time they were finished the Sabbath had begun, so they rested as required by the law.

THE RESURRECTION

But very early on Sunday morning the women went to the tomb, taking the spices they had prepared.

MARY MAGDALENE

Mary of Magdala not only traveled with Jesus but also contributed to the needs of the group. She was present at the Crucifixion and was on her way to anoint Jesus' body on Sunday morning when she discovered the empty tomb. Mary was the first to see Jesus after his resurrection.

Mary Magdalene is a heartwarming example of thankful living. Her life was miraculously freed by Jesus when he drove seven demons out of her. In every glimpse we have of her, she was acting out her appreciation for the freedom Christ had given her. That freedom allowed her to stand under Christ's cross when all the disciples except John were hiding in fear.

Mary's faith was direct and genuine. She was more eager to believe and obey than to understand everything. Jesus honored her childlike faith by appearing to her first and by entrusting her with the message of his resurrection.

+ **STRENGTHS AND ACCOMPLISHMENTS:** Contributed to the needs of Jesus and his disciples

One of the few faithful followers present at Jesus' death on the cross

First to see the risen Christ

+ **WEAKNESS AND MISTAKE:** Jesus had to drive seven demons out of her

+ **LESSONS FROM HER LIFE:** Those who are obedient grow in understanding

Jesus relates to women as he created them—as equal reflectors of God's image

+ **VITAL STATISTICS:** Where: Magdala and Jerusalem

Occupation: We are not told, but she seems to have been wealthy

They found that the stone had been rolled away from the entrance. So they went in, but they didn't find the body of the Lord Jesus. As they stood there puzzled, two men suddenly appeared to them, clothed in dazzling robes.

The women were terrified and bowed with their faces to the ground. Then the men asked, "Why are you looking among the dead for someone who is alive? He isn't here! He is risen from the dead! Remember what he told you back in Galilee, that the Son of Man must be betrayed into the hands of sinful men and be crucified, and that he would rise again on the third day."

Then they remembered that he had said this. So they rushed back from the tomb to tell his eleven disciples—and everyone else—what had happened. It was Mary Magdalene, Joanna, Mary the mother of James, and several other women who told the apostles what had happened. But the story sounded like nonsense to the men, so they didn't believe it. However, Peter jumped up and ran to the tomb to look. Stooping, he peered in and saw the empty linen wrappings; then he went home again, wondering what had happened.

The Walk to Emmaus

That same day two of Jesus' followers were walking to the village of Emmaus, seven miles from Jerusalem. As they walked along they were talking about everything that had happened. As they talked and discussed these things, Jesus himself suddenly came and began walking with them. But God kept them from recognizing him.

He asked them, "What are you discussing so intently as you walk along?"

They stopped short, sadness written across their faces. Then one of them, Cleopas, replied, "You must be the only person in Jerusalem who hasn't heard about all the things that have happened there the last few days."

"What things?" Jesus asked.

"The things that happened to Jesus, the man from Nazareth," they said. "He was a prophet who did powerful miracles, and he was a mighty teacher in the eyes of God and all the people. But our leading priests and other religious leaders handed him over to be condemned to death, and they crucified him. We had hoped he was the Messiah who had come to rescue Israel. This all happened three days ago.

"Then some women from our group of his followers were at his tomb early this morning, and they came back with an amazing report. They said his body was missing, and they had seen angels who told them Jesus is alive! Some of our men ran out to see, and sure enough, his body was gone, just as the women had said."

Then Jesus said to them, "You foolish people! You find it so hard to believe all that the prophets wrote in the Scriptures. Wasn't it clearly predicted that the Messiah would have to suffer all these things before entering his glory?" Then Jesus took them through the writings of Moses and all the prophets, explaining from all the Scriptures the things concerning himself.

By this time they were nearing Emmaus and the end of their journey. Jesus acted as if he were going on, but they begged him, "Stay the night with us, since it is getting late." So he went home with them. As they sat down to eat, he took the bread and blessed it. Then he broke it and gave it to them. Suddenly, their eyes were opened, and they recognized him. And at that moment he disappeared!

They said to each other, "Didn't our hearts burn within us as he talked with us on the road and explained the Scriptures to us?" And within the hour they were on their way back to Jerusalem. There they found the eleven disciples and the others who had gathered with them, who said, "The Lord has really risen! He appeared to Peter."

Jesus Appears to the Disciples

Then the two from Emmaus told their story of how Jesus had appeared to them as they were walking along the road, and how they had recognized him as he was breaking the bread. And just as they were telling about it, Jesus himself was suddenly standing there among them. "Peace be with you," he said. But the whole group was startled and frightened, thinking they were seeing a ghost!

"Why are you frightened?" he asked. "Why are your hearts filled with doubt? Look at my hands. Look at my feet. You can see that it's really me. Touch me and make sure that I am not a ghost, because ghosts don't have bodies, as you see that

I do." As he spoke, he showed them his hands and his feet.

Still they stood there in disbelief, filled with joy and wonder. Then he asked them, "Do you have anything here to eat?" They gave him a piece of broiled fish, and he ate it as they watched.

Then he said, "When I was with you before, I told you that everything written about me in the law of Moses and the prophets and in the Psalms must be fulfilled." Then he opened their minds to understand the Scriptures. And he said, "Yes, it was written long ago that the Messiah would suffer and die and rise from the dead on the third day. It was also written that this message would be proclaimed in the authority of his name to all the nations, beginning in Jerusalem: 'There is forgiveness of sins for all who repent.' You are witnesses of all these things.

"And now I will send the Holy Spirit, just as my Father promised. But stay here in the city until the Holy Spirit comes and fills you with power from heaven."

THE ASCENSION

Then Jesus led them to Bethany, and lifting his hands to heaven, he blessed them. While he was blessing them, he left them and was taken up to heaven. So they worshiped him and then returned to Jerusalem filled with great joy. And they spent all of their time in the Temple, praising God.

JESUS' CRUCIFIXION AND RESURRECTION

It's a turn of phrase that crops up occasionally in our vernacular: "Such and such is the crux of the matter." *Crux*, which means "the most important thing," is the Latin word for "cross." That provides a nice play on words when it comes to Christian theology: "The cross of Christ is the crux of Christianity." Without the cross of Christ, Christianity loses its redemptive message.

The story of the cross is not just a history lesson that we read about in a book. It's a reminder to each of us that our sin—our falling short of God's glory—is the very reason that Jesus Christ died on the cross:

- "Christ has rescued us from the curse pronounced by the law. When he was hung on the cross, he took upon himself the curse for our wrongdoing. For it is written in the Scriptures, 'Cursed is everyone who is hung on a tree'" (Galatians 3:13).
- "He canceled the record of the charges against us and took it away by nailing it to the cross" (Colossians 2:14).
- "He personally carried our sins in his body on the cross so that we can be dead to sin and live for what is right. By his wounds you are healed" (1 Peter 2:24).

God picked the best that heaven could offer, his perfect and only Son, and sent him to earth to pay the penalty for our sins. The cross is the crux of Christ's work—and our lives—because it is the way God has chosen to bring us back into a loving relationship with him.

The crucifixion of Christ is inseparable from the resurrection of Christ. One without the other is only half of the story of redemption. The apostle Paul said it this way:

"If Christ has not been raised, then all our preaching is useless, and your faith is useless" (1 Corinthians 15:14).

But Christ *has* been raised, and his resurrection has wonderful implications for all of our lives (1 Corinthians 15:20). When we come to believe the Resurrection, it will change our pasts, our presents, and our futures.

THE RESURRECTION IS ABOUT OUR PAST

The pain of an unforgiven life can be unbearable. Some people go mad trying to deal with the shame and guilt of the past. Others experience an inescapable, low-level throb reminding them of the ways they have wounded others and sinned against God. In his book *The Contemporary Christian*, John Stott writes, "Forgiveness is one of our most basic needs and one of God's best gifts. . . . We all have a skeleton or two in some dark cupboard, memories of things we have thought, said or done, of which in our better moments we are thoroughly ashamed. Our conscience nags, condemns, torments us."[1]

The wonderful news of the gospel is that Jesus died and was raised to life to free us from the guilt and condemnation of our past. He was "handed over to die because of our sins, and he was raised to life to make us right with God" (Romans 4:25).

The bill for our debt of sin was paid at the Cross, and the receipt for that bill is the Resurrection! If Jesus had not been raised from the dead, his death would have been in vain, and we would still bear the weight and guilt of our sin (1 Corinthians 15:17). But through his resurrection, we are assured that we can have free and full forgiveness for all our sins.

THE RESURRECTION IS ABOUT OUR PRESENT

In Paul's letter to the Ephesians, he makes an astounding statement. In his prayer for the Ephesian believers, he asks God that these new Christians might know the greatness of God's power in their lives each day, and then he says that this is the same power that raised Christ from the dead and seated him at God's right hand in heaven (Ephesians 1:19-20).

In other words, the power that brought Jesus back to

life on that first Easter is available to us, too, when we put our trust in him. It is through this power that we are raised from spiritual death and given new life. It is this power that takes people who have no interest in the things of God and makes them into students of God's Word and followers of Jesus Christ.

When you become a Christian, it means you begin experiencing the power of the Resurrection today. God's Spirit will transform who you are and how you respond to the challenges of life. And although your circumstances might not change, your heart will. Instead of being filled with fear, anger, or jealousy, your life will begin to be characterized by love, joy, and peace. The Resurrection is not just about your past; it is also about your present!

THE RESURRECTION IS ABOUT OUR FUTURE

Listen to these words concerning the resurrection of Jesus Christ and our hope for the future: "All praise to God, the Father of our Lord Jesus Christ. It is by his great mercy that we have been born again, because God raised Jesus Christ from the dead. Now we live with great expectation, and we have a priceless inheritance—an inheritance that is kept in heaven for you, pure and undefiled, beyond the reach of change and decay. And through your faith, God is protecting you by his power until you receive this salvation, which is ready to be revealed on the last day for all to see" (1 Peter 1:3-5).

No matter how dark our situations in life might be, our hope is anchored in Jesus Christ and his victory over the grave. Because he is alive, our hope is alive too, and we can look forward to a special inheritance that can't be destroyed, defiled, or diminished, since it is reserved for us in heaven. Through the Resurrection, our eternal inheritance is secure. Nothing can keep us from that hope.

The resurrection of Jesus Christ is the guarantee of our future resurrection. Because Jesus was victorious over the grave, we, too, have confidence that we will be raised up in triumph over death.

Christ's death and resurrection force us to choose what we believe about the biggest issues of life—about sin and salvation, life and death. It truly is a crossroads that demands a decision. I urge you to place your trust in the life, death, and resurrection of Jesus Christ. When you do, you can be sure that your past is forgiven—your failures are not fatal. Your present is meaningful—your life is not futile. Your future is secured—your death is not final.

THE BOOK OF ACTS

CHAPTER
ONE

THE PROMISE OF THE HOLY SPIRIT

In my first book I told you, Theophilus, about everything Jesus began to do and teach until the day he was taken up to heaven after giving his chosen apostles further instructions through the Holy Spirit. During the forty days after he suffered and died, he appeared to the apostles from time to time, and he proved to them in many ways that he was actually alive. And he talked to them about the Kingdom of God.

Once when he was eating with them, he commanded them, "Do not leave Jerusalem until the Father sends you the gift he promised, as I told you before. John baptized with water, but in just a few days you will be baptized with the Holy Spirit."

The Ascension of Jesus

So when the apostles were with Jesus, they kept asking him, "Lord, has the time come for you to free Israel and restore our kingdom?"

He replied, "The Father alone has the authority to set those dates and times, and they are not for you to know. But you will receive power when the Holy Spirit comes upon you. And you will be my witnesses, telling people about me everywhere—in Jerusalem, throughout Judea, in Samaria, and to the ends of the earth."

After saying this, he was taken up into a cloud while they were watching, and they could no longer see him. As they strained to see him rising into heaven, two white-robed men suddenly stood among them. "Men of Galilee," they said, "why are you standing here staring into heaven? Jesus has been taken from you into heaven, but someday he will return from heaven in the same way you saw him go!"

Matthias Replaces Judas

Then the apostles returned to Jerusalem from the Mount of Olives, a distance of half a mile. When they arrived, they went to the upstairs room of the house where they were staying.

Here are the names of those who were present: Peter, John, James, Andrew, Philip, Thomas, Bartholomew, Matthew, James (son of Alphaeus), Simon (the Zealot), and Judas (son of James). They all met together and were constantly united in prayer, along with Mary the mother of Jesus, several other women, and the brothers of Jesus.

LUKE

Although we know few facts of his life, Luke has left us a strong impression of himself by what he wrote. In his Gospel, he emphasizes Jesus Christ's compassion. He vividly recorded both the power demonstrated by Christ's life and the care with which Christ treated people. Luke's writing in Acts is full of sharp verbal pictures of real people caught up in the greatest events of history.

Luke was also a doctor. He had a traveling medical practice as Paul's companion. Since the gospel was often welcomed with whips and stones, the doctor was undoubtedly never lacking patients.

God made special use of Luke as the historian of the early church. Repeatedly, the details of Luke's descriptions have been proven accurate. The first words in his Gospel indicate his interest in the truth.

And yet Luke accomplished all this while staying out of the spotlight. Perhaps his greatest example to us is the challenge to greatness even when we are not the center of attention.

+ **STRENGTHS AND ACCOMPLISHMENTS:** A humble, faithful, and useful companion of Paul

A well-educated and trained physician

A careful and exact historian

Writer of both the Gospel of Luke and the book of Acts

+ **LESSONS FROM HIS LIFE:** The words we leave behind will be a lasting picture of who we are

Excellence is shown by how we work when no one is noticing

+ **VITAL STATISTICS:** Where: Probably met Paul in Troas

Occupations: Doctor, historian, traveling companion

During this time, when about 120 believers were together in one place, Peter stood up and addressed them. "Brothers," he said, "the Scriptures had to be fulfilled concerning Judas, who guided those who arrested Jesus. This was predicted long ago by the Holy Spirit, speaking through King David. Judas was one of us and shared in the ministry with us."

(Judas had bought a field with the money he received for his treachery. Falling headfirst there, his body split open, spilling out all his intestines. The news of his death spread to all the people of Jerusalem, and they gave the place the Aramaic name *Akeldama*, which means "Field of Blood.")

Peter continued, "This was written in the book of Psalms, where it says, 'Let his home become desolate, with no one living in it.' It also says, 'Let someone else take his position.'

"So now we must choose a replacement for Judas from among the men who were with us the entire time we were traveling with the Lord Jesus—from the time he was baptized by John until the day he was taken from us. Whoever is chosen will join us as a witness of Jesus' resurrection."

So they nominated two men: Joseph called Barsabbas (also known as Justus) and Matthias. Then they all prayed, "O Lord, you know every heart. Show us which of these men you have chosen as an apostle to replace Judas in this ministry, for he has deserted us and gone where he belongs." Then they cast lots, and Matthias was selected to become an apostle with the other eleven.

CHAPTER
TWO

THE HOLY SPIRIT COMES

On the day of Pentecost all the believers were meeting together in one place. Suddenly, there was a sound from heaven like the roaring of a mighty windstorm, and it filled the house where they were sitting. Then, what looked like flames or tongues of fire appeared and settled on each of them. And everyone present was filled with the Holy Spirit and began speaking in other languages, as the Holy Spirit gave them this ability.

At that time there were devout Jews from every nation living in Jerusalem. When they heard the loud noise, everyone came running, and they were bewildered to hear their own languages being spoken by the believers.

They were completely amazed. "How can this be?" they exclaimed. "These people are all from

Galilee, and yet we hear them speaking in our own native languages! Here we are—Parthians, Medes, Elamites, people from Mesopotamia, Judea, Cappadocia, Pontus, the province of Asia, Phrygia, Pamphylia, Egypt, and the areas of Libya around Cyrene, visitors from Rome (both Jews and converts to Judaism), Cretans, and Arabs. And we all hear these people speaking in our own languages about the wonderful things God has done!" They stood there amazed and perplexed. "What can this mean?" they asked each other.

But others in the crowd ridiculed them, saying, "They're just drunk, that's all!"

PETER PREACHES TO THE CROWD

Then Peter stepped forward with the eleven other apostles and shouted to the crowd, "Listen carefully, all of you, fellow Jews and residents of Jerusalem! Make no mistake about this. These people are not drunk, as some of you are assuming. Nine o'clock in the morning is much too early for that. No, what you see was predicted long ago by the prophet Joel:

'In the last days,' God says,
'I will pour out my Spirit upon all people.
Your sons and daughters will prophesy.
Your young men will see visions,
and your old men will dream dreams.
In those days I will pour out my Spirit
even on my servants—men and women alike—
and they will prophesy.

PETER

Jesus' first words to Simon Peter were "Come, follow me" (Mark 1:17). His last words to him were "Follow me" (John 21:22). Every step of the way between those two challenges, Peter never wavered in his desire to follow—even though he often stumbled.

When Jesus entered Peter's life, this plain fisherman became a new person with new goals and priorities. He did not become a perfect person, however. We may wonder what Jesus saw in Simon that made him greet this potential disciple with a new name: Peter—the "rock." Impulsive Peter certainly didn't act like a rock much of the time. But Jesus was looking for real people—followers who could be changed by his love. Then he sent them out to communicate that his acceptance was available to anyone—even to those who often fail.

+ **STRENGTHS AND ACCOMPLISHMENTS:** Became the recognized leader among Jesus' disciples—one of the inner group of three (along with James and John)

Was the first great voice of the gospel during and after Pentecost

Probably knew Mark and gave him information for the Gospel of Mark

Wrote 1 and 2 Peter

+ **WEAKNESSES AND MISTAKES:** Often spoke without thinking; was brash and impulsive

During Jesus' trial, denied three times that he even knew Jesus

+ **LESSONS FROM HIS LIFE:** God's faithfulness can compensate for our greatest unfaithfulness

It is better to be a follower who sometimes fails than one who fails to follow

+ **VITAL STATISTICS:** Occupations: Fisherman, disciple

Relatives: Father: John. Brother: Andrew.

And I will cause wonders in the heavens above
　　and signs on the earth below—
　　blood and fire and clouds of smoke.
The sun will become dark,
　　and the moon will turn blood red
　　before that great and glorious day of the
　　　　LORD *arrives.*
But everyone who calls on the name of the LORD
　　will be saved.'

"People of Israel, listen! God publicly endorsed Jesus the Nazarene by doing powerful miracles, wonders, and signs through him, as you well know. But God knew what would happen, and his prearranged plan was carried out when Jesus was betrayed. With the help of lawless Gentiles, you nailed him to a cross and killed him. But God released him from the horrors of death and raised him back to life, for death could not keep him in its grip. King David said this about him:

'I see that the LORD *is always with me.*
　　I will not be shaken, for he is right beside me.
No wonder my heart is glad,
　　and my tongue shouts his praises!
　　My body rests in hope.
For you will not leave my soul among the dead
　　or allow your Holy One to rot in the grave.
You have shown me the way of life,
　　and you will fill me with the joy of your
　　　　presence.'

"Dear brothers, think about this! You can be sure that the patriarch David wasn't referring to himself, for he died and was buried, and his tomb is still here among us. But he was a prophet, and he knew God had promised with an oath that one of David's own descendants would sit on his throne. David was looking into the future and speaking of the Messiah's resurrection. He was saying that God would not leave him among the dead or allow his body to rot in the grave.

"God raised Jesus from the dead, and we are all witnesses of this. Now he is exalted to the place of highest honor in heaven, at God's right hand. And the Father, as he had promised, gave him the Holy Spirit to pour out upon us, just as you see and hear today. For David himself never ascended into heaven, yet he said,

'The LORD said to my Lord,
    "Sit in the place of honor at my right hand
until I humble your enemies,
    making them a footstool under your feet."'

"So let everyone in Israel know for certain that God has made this Jesus, whom you crucified, to be both Lord and Messiah!"

Peter's words pierced their hearts, and they said to him and to the other apostles, "Brothers, what should we do?"

Peter replied, "Each of you must repent of your sins and turn to God, and be baptized in the name of Jesus Christ for the forgiveness of your sins. Then you will receive the gift of the Holy Spirit. This promise is to you, to your children, and to those far away—all who have been called by the Lord our God." Then Peter continued preaching for a long time, strongly urging all his listeners, "Save yourselves from this crooked generation!"

Those who believed what Peter said were baptized and added to the church that day—about 3,000 in all.

The Believers Form a Community

All the believers devoted themselves to the apostles' teaching, and to fellowship, and to sharing in meals (including the Lord's Supper), and to prayer.

A deep sense of awe came over them all, and the apostles performed many miraculous signs and wonders. And all the believers met together in one place and shared everything they had. They sold their property and possessions and shared the money with those in need. They worshiped together at the Temple each day, met in homes for the Lord's Supper, and shared their meals with great joy and generosity—all the while praising God and enjoying the goodwill of all the people. And each day the Lord added to their fellowship those who were being saved.

CHAPTER
THREE

PETER HEALS A CRIPPLED BEGGAR

Peter and John went to the Temple one afternoon to take part in the three o'clock prayer service. As they approached the Temple, a man lame from birth was being carried in. Each day he was put beside the Temple gate, the one called the Beautiful Gate, so he could beg from the people going into the Temple. When he saw Peter and John about to enter, he asked them for some money.

Peter and John looked at him intently, and Peter said, "Look at us!" The lame man looked at them eagerly, expecting some money. But Peter said, "I don't have any silver or gold for you. But I'll give you what I have. In the name of Jesus Christ the Nazarene, get up and walk!"

Then Peter took the lame man by the right hand and helped him up. And as he did, the man's feet and ankles were instantly healed and strengthened. He jumped up, stood on his feet, and began to walk! Then, walking, leaping, and praising God, he went into the Temple with them.

All the people saw him walking and heard him praising God. When they realized he was the lame beggar they had seen so often at the Beautiful Gate, they were absolutely astounded! They all rushed out in amazement to Solomon's Colonnade, where the man was holding tightly to Peter and John.

PETER PREACHES IN THE TEMPLE

Peter saw his opportunity and addressed the crowd. "People of Israel," he said, "what is so surprising about this? And why stare at us as though we had made this man walk by our own power or godliness? For it is the God of Abraham, Isaac, and Jacob—the God of all our ancestors—who has brought glory to his servant Jesus by doing this. This is the same Jesus whom you handed over and rejected before Pilate, despite Pilate's decision to release him. You rejected this holy, righteous one and instead demanded the release of a murderer. You killed the author of life, but God raised him from the dead. And we are witnesses of this fact!

"Through faith in the name of Jesus, this man was healed—and you know how crippled he was before. Faith in Jesus' name has healed him before your very eyes.

"Friends, I realize that what you and your leaders did to Jesus was done in ignorance. But God was fulfilling what all the prophets had foretold about the Messiah—that he must suffer these things. Now repent of your sins and turn to God, so that your sins may be wiped away. Then times of refreshment will come from the presence of the Lord, and he will again send you Jesus, your appointed Messiah. For he must remain in heaven until the time for the final restoration of all things, as God promised long ago through his holy prophets. Moses said, 'The LORD your God will raise up for you a Prophet like me from among your own people. Listen carefully to everything he tells you.' Then Moses said, 'Anyone who will not listen to that Prophet will be completely cut off from God's people.'

"Starting with Samuel, every prophet spoke about what is happening today. You are the children of those prophets, and you are included in the covenant God promised to your ancestors. For God said to Abraham, 'Through your descendants all the families on earth will be blessed.' When God raised up his servant, Jesus, he sent him first to you people of Israel, to bless you by turning each of you back from your sinful ways."

CHAPTER
FOUR

PETER AND JOHN BEFORE THE COUNCIL

While Peter and John were speaking to the people, they were confronted by the priests, the captain of the Temple guard, and some of the Sadducees. These leaders were very disturbed that Peter and John were teaching the people that through Jesus there is a resurrection of the dead. They arrested them and, since it was already evening, put them in jail until morning. But many of the people who heard their message believed it, so the number of believers now totaled about 5,000 men, not counting women and children.

The next day the council of all the rulers and elders and teachers of religious law met in Jerusalem. Annas the high priest was there, along with Caiaphas, John, Alexander, and other relatives of the high priest. They brought in the two disciples and demanded, "By what power, or in whose name, have you done this?"

Then Peter, filled with the Holy Spirit, said to them, "Rulers and elders of our people, are we being questioned today because we've done a good deed for a crippled man? Do you want to know how he was healed? Let me clearly state to all of you and to all the people of Israel that he was healed by the powerful name of Jesus Christ the Nazarene, the man you crucified but whom God raised from the dead. For Jesus is the one referred to in the Scriptures, where it says,

*'The stone that you builders rejected
has now become the cornerstone.'*

There is salvation in no one else! God has given no other name under heaven by which we must be saved."

The members of the council were amazed when they saw the boldness of Peter and John, for they could see that they were ordinary men with no special training in the Scriptures. They also recognized them as men who had been with Jesus. But since they could see the man who had been healed standing right there among them, there was nothing the council could say. So they ordered Peter and John out of the council chamber and conferred among themselves.

"What should we do with these men?" they asked each other. "We can't deny that they have performed a miraculous sign, and everybody in Jerusalem knows about it. But to keep them from spreading their propaganda any further, we must warn them not to speak to anyone in Jesus' name again." So they called the apostles back in and commanded them never again to speak or teach in the name of Jesus.

But Peter and John replied, "Do you think God wants us to obey you rather than him? We cannot stop telling about everything we have seen and heard."

The council then threatened them further, but they finally let them go because they didn't know how to punish them without starting a riot. For everyone was praising God for this miraculous sign—the healing of a man who had been lame for more than forty years.

THE BELIEVERS PRAY FOR COURAGE

As soon as they were freed, Peter and John returned to the other believers and told them what the leading priests and elders had said. When they heard the report, all the believers lifted their voices together in prayer to God: "O Sovereign Lord, Creator of heaven and earth, the sea, and everything in them—you spoke long ago by the Holy Spirit through our ancestor David, your servant, saying,

> *'Why were the nations so angry?*
> *Why did they waste their time with futile plans?*
> *The kings of the earth prepared for battle;*
> *the rulers gathered together*
> *against the LORD*
> *and against his Messiah.'*

"In fact, this has happened here in this very city! For Herod Antipas, Pontius Pilate the governor, the Gentiles, and the people of Israel were all united against Jesus, your holy servant, whom you anointed. But everything they did was determined beforehand according to your will. And now, O Lord, hear their threats, and give us, your servants, great boldness in preaching your word. Stretch out your hand with healing power; may miraculous signs and wonders be done through the name of your holy servant Jesus."

After this prayer, the meeting place shook, and they were all filled with the Holy Spirit. Then they preached the word of God with boldness.

The Believers Share Their Possessions

All the believers were united in heart and mind. And they felt that what they owned was not their own, so they shared everything they had. The apostles testified powerfully to the resurrection of the Lord Jesus, and God's great blessing was upon them all. There were no needy people among them, because those who owned land or houses would sell them and bring the money to the apostles to give to those in need.

For instance, there was Joseph, the one the apostles nicknamed Barnabas (which means "Son of Encouragement"). He was from the tribe of Levi and came from the island of Cyprus. He sold a field he owned and brought the money to the apostles.

CHAPTER
FIVE

ANANIAS AND SAPPHIRA

But there was a certain man named Ananias who, with his wife, Sapphira, sold some property. He brought part of the money to the apostles, claiming it was the full amount. With his wife's consent, he kept the rest.

Then Peter said, "Ananias, why have you let Satan fill your heart? You lied to the Holy Spirit, and you kept some of the money for yourself. The property was yours to sell or not sell, as you wished. And after selling it, the money was also yours to give away. How could you do a thing like this? You weren't lying to us but to God!"

As soon as Ananias heard these words, he fell to the floor and died. Everyone who heard about it was terrified. Then some young men got up, wrapped him in a sheet, and took him out and buried him.

About three hours later his wife came in, not knowing what had happened. Peter asked her, "Was this the price you and your husband received for your land?"

"Yes," she replied, "that was the price."

And Peter said, "How could the two of you even think of conspiring to test the Spirit of the Lord like this? The young men who buried your husband are just outside the door, and they will carry you out, too."

Instantly, she fell to the floor and died. When the young men came in and saw that she was dead, they carried her out and buried her beside her husband. Great fear gripped the entire church and everyone else who heard what had happened.

The Apostles Heal Many

The apostles were performing many miraculous signs and wonders among the people. And all the believers were meeting regularly at the Temple in the area known as Solomon's Colonnade. But no one else dared to join them, even though all the people had high regard for them. Yet more and more people believed and were brought to the Lord—crowds of both men and women. As a result of the apostles' work, sick people were brought out into the streets on beds and mats so that Peter's shadow might fall across some of them as he went by. Crowds came from the villages around Jerusalem, bringing their sick and those possessed by evil spirits, and they were all healed.

THE APOSTLES MEET OPPOSITION

The high priest and his officials, who were Sadducees, were filled with jealousy. They arrested the apostles and put them in the public jail. But an angel of the Lord came at night, opened the gates of the jail, and brought them out. Then he told them, "Go to the Temple and give the people this message of life!"

So at daybreak the apostles entered the Temple, as they were told, and immediately began teaching.

When the high priest and his officials arrived, they convened the high council—the full assembly of the elders of Israel. Then they sent for the apostles to be brought from the jail for trial. But when the Temple guards went to the jail, the men were gone. So they returned to the council and reported, "The jail was securely locked, with the guards standing outside, but when we opened the gates, no one was there!"

When the captain of the Temple guard and the leading priests heard this, they were perplexed, wondering where it would all end. Then someone arrived with startling news: "The men you put in jail are standing in the Temple, teaching the people!"

The captain went with his Temple guards and arrested the apostles, but without violence, for they were afraid the people would stone them. Then they brought the apostles before the high council, where the high priest confronted them. "We gave you strict orders never again to teach in this man's name!" he said. "Instead, you have filled all Jerusalem with your teaching about him, and you want to make us responsible for his death!"

But Peter and the apostles replied, "We must obey God rather than any human authority. The God of our ancestors raised Jesus from the dead after you killed him by hanging him on a cross. Then God put him in the place of honor at his right hand as Prince and Savior. He did this so the people of Israel would repent of their sins and be forgiven. We are witnesses of these things and so is the Holy Spirit, who is given by God to those who obey him."

When they heard this, the high council was furious and decided to kill them. But one member, a Pharisee named Gamaliel, who was an expert in religious law and respected by all the people, stood up and ordered that the men be sent outside the council chamber for a while. Then he said to his colleagues, "Men of Israel, take care what you are planning to do to these men! Some time ago there was that fellow Theudas, who pretended to be someone great. About 400 others joined him, but he was killed, and all his followers went their various ways. The whole movement came to nothing. After him, at the time of the census, there was Judas of Galilee. He got people to follow him, but he was killed, too, and all his followers were scattered.

"So my advice is, leave these men alone. Let them go. If they are planning and doing these things merely on their own, it will soon be overthrown. But if it is from God, you will not be able to overthrow them. You may even find yourselves fighting against God!"

The others accepted his advice. They called in the apostles and had them flogged. Then they ordered them never again to speak in the name of Jesus, and they let them go.

The apostles left the high council rejoicing that God had counted them worthy to suffer disgrace for the name of Jesus. And every day, in the Temple and from house to house, they continued to teach and preach this message: "Jesus is the Messiah."

CHAPTER
SIX

SEVEN MEN CHOSEN TO SERVE

But as the believers rapidly multiplied, there were rumblings of discontent. The Greek-speaking believers complained about the Hebrew-speaking believers, saying that their widows were being discriminated against in the daily distribution of food.

So the Twelve called a meeting of all the believers. They said, "We apostles should spend our time teaching the word of God, not running a food program. And so, brothers, select seven men who are well respected and are full of the Spirit and wisdom. We will give them this responsibility. Then we apostles can spend our time in prayer and teaching the word."

Everyone liked this idea, and they chose the following: Stephen (a man full of faith and the Holy Spirit), Philip, Procorus, Nicanor, Timon,

Parmenas, and Nicolas of Antioch (an earlier convert to the Jewish faith). These seven were presented to the apostles, who prayed for them as they laid their hands on them.

So God's message continued to spread. The number of believers greatly increased in Jerusalem, and many of the Jewish priests were converted, too.

STEPHEN IS ARRESTED

Stephen, a man full of God's grace and power, performed amazing miracles and signs among the people. But one day some men from the Synagogue of Freed Slaves, as it was called, started to debate with him. They were Jews from Cyrene, Alexandria, Cilicia, and the province of Asia. None of them could stand against the wisdom and the Spirit with which Stephen spoke.

So they persuaded some men to lie about Stephen, saying, "We heard him blaspheme Moses, and even God." This roused the people, the elders, and the teachers of religious law. So they arrested Stephen and brought him before the high council.

The lying witnesses said, "This man is always speaking against the holy Temple and against the law of Moses. We have heard him say that this Jesus of Nazareth will destroy the Temple and change the customs Moses handed down to us."

At this point everyone in the high council stared at Stephen, because his face became as bright as an angel's.

CHAPTER
SEVEN

STEPHEN ADDRESSES THE COUNCIL

Then the high priest asked Stephen, "Are these accusations true?"

This was Stephen's reply: "Brothers and fathers, listen to me. Our glorious God appeared to our ancestor Abraham in Mesopotamia before he settled in Haran. God told him, 'Leave your native land and your relatives, and come into the land that I will show you.' So Abraham left the land of the Chaldeans and lived in Haran until his father died. Then God brought him here to the land where you now live.

"But God gave him no inheritance here, not even one square foot of land. God did promise, however, that eventually the whole land would belong to Abraham and his descendants—even though he had no children yet. God also told him that his descendants would live in a foreign land, where they would be oppressed as slaves for 400 years. 'But I will punish the nation that enslaves them,' God said, 'and in the end they will come out and worship me here in this place.'

"God also gave Abraham the covenant of circumcision at that time. So when Abraham became the father of Isaac, he circumcised him on the eighth day. And the practice was continued when Isaac became the father of Jacob, and when Jacob became the father of the twelve patriarchs of the Israelite nation.

"These patriarchs were jealous of their brother Joseph, and they sold him to be a slave in Egypt. But God was with him and rescued him from all his troubles. And God gave him favor before Pharaoh, king of Egypt. God also gave Joseph unusual wisdom, so that Pharaoh appointed him governor over all of Egypt and put him in charge of the palace.

"But a famine came upon Egypt and Canaan. There was great misery, and our ancestors ran out of food. Jacob heard that there was still grain in Egypt, so he sent his sons—our ancestors—to buy some. The second time they went, Joseph revealed his identity to his brothers, and they were introduced to Pharaoh. Then Joseph sent for his father, Jacob, and all his relatives to come to Egypt, seventy-five persons in all. So Jacob went to Egypt. He died there, as did our ancestors. Their bodies were taken to Shechem and buried in the tomb Abraham had bought for a certain price from Hamor's sons in Shechem.

"As the time drew near when God would fulfill

STEPHEN

Besides being a good administrator, Stephen was also a powerful speaker. When confronted by various antagonistic groups, Stephen made a convincing defense before the Jewish high council, presenting a summary of the Jews' own history, and made powerful applications that stung his listeners. As a result, members of the council stoned him to death while he prayed for their forgiveness. His final words show how much like Jesus he had become in just a short time. His death had a lasting impact on young Saul (Paul) of Tarsus, who would move from being a violent persecutor of Christians to being one of the greatest champions of the gospel the church has known.

Stephen's life is a continual challenge to all Christians. Because he was the first to die for the faith, his sacrifice raises questions: How many risks do we take in being Jesus' followers? Would we be willing to die for him? Are we really willing to live for him?

+ **STRENGTHS AND ACCOMPLISHMENTS:** One of seven leaders chosen to supervise food distribution to the needy in the early church

Known for his faith, wisdom, grace, and power; also known for the Spirit's presence in his life

Outstanding leader, teacher, and debater

First to give his life for the gospel

+ **LESSONS FROM HIS LIFE:** Striving for excellence in small assignments prepares one for greater responsibilities

Real understanding of God always leads to practical and compassionate actions toward people

+ **VITAL STATISTICS:** Occupation: Organizer of food distribution for the early church

his promise to Abraham, the number of our people in Egypt greatly increased. But then a new king came to the throne of Egypt who knew nothing about Joseph. This king exploited our people and oppressed them, forcing parents to abandon their newborn babies so they would die.

"At that time Moses was born—a beautiful child in God's eyes. His parents cared for him at home for three months. When they had to abandon him, Pharaoh's daughter adopted him and raised him as her own son. Moses was taught all the wisdom of the Egyptians, and he was powerful in both speech and action.

"One day when Moses was forty years old, he decided to visit his relatives, the people of Israel. He saw an Egyptian mistreating an Israelite. So Moses came to the man's defense and avenged him, killing the Egyptian. Moses assumed his fellow Israelites would realize that God had sent him to rescue them, but they didn't.

"The next day he visited them again and saw two men of Israel fighting. He tried to be a peacemaker. 'Men,' he said, 'you are brothers. Why are you fighting each other?'

"But the man in the wrong pushed Moses aside. 'Who made you a ruler and judge over us?' he asked. 'Are you going to kill me as you killed that Egyptian yesterday?' When Moses heard that, he fled the country and lived as a foreigner in the land of Midian. There his two sons were born.

"Forty years later, in the desert near Mount Sinai, an angel appeared to Moses in the flame of a burning bush. When Moses saw it, he was amazed at the sight. As he went to take a closer look, the voice of the LORD called out to him, 'I am the God of your ancestors—the God of Abraham, Isaac, and Jacob.' Moses shook with terror and did not dare to look.

"Then the LORD said to him, 'Take off your sandals, for you are standing on holy ground. I have certainly seen the oppression of my people in Egypt. I have heard their groans and have come down to rescue them. Now go, for I am sending you back to Egypt.'

"So God sent back the same man his people had previously rejected when they demanded, 'Who made you a ruler and judge over us?' Through the angel who appeared to him in the burning bush, God sent Moses to be their ruler and savior. And by means of many wonders and miraculous signs, he led them out of Egypt, through the Red Sea, and through the wilderness for forty years.

"Moses himself told the people of Israel, 'God will raise up for you a Prophet like me from among your own people.' Moses was with our ancestors, the assembly of God's people in the wilderness, when the angel spoke to him at Mount Sinai. And there Moses received life-giving words to pass on to us.

"But our ancestors refused to listen to Moses. They rejected him and wanted to return to Egypt. They told Aaron, 'Make us some gods who can lead us, for we don't know what has become of this Moses, who brought us out of Egypt.' So they made an idol shaped like a calf, and they sacrificed to it and celebrated over this thing they had made. Then God turned away from them and abandoned them to serve the stars of heaven as their gods! In the book of the prophets it is written,

> *'Was it to me you were bringing sacrifices and*
> *offerings*
> *during those forty years in the wilderness,*
> *Israel?*
> *No, you carried your pagan gods—*
> *the shrine of Molech,*
> *the star of your god Rephan,*
> *and the images you made to worship them.*
> *So I will send you into exile*
> *as far away as Babylon.'*

"Our ancestors carried the Tabernacle with them through the wilderness. It was constructed according to the plan God had shown to Moses. Years later, when Joshua led our ancestors in battle against the nations that God drove out of this land, the Tabernacle was taken with them into their new territory. And it stayed there until the time of King David.

"David found favor with God and asked for the privilege of building a permanent Temple for the God of Jacob. But it was Solomon who actually built it. However, the Most High doesn't live in temples made by human hands. As the prophet says,

> *'Heaven is my throne,*
> *and the earth is my footstool.*

Could you build me a temple as good as that?'
asks the LORD.
'Could you build me such a resting place?
Didn't my hands make both heaven
and earth?'

"You stubborn people! You are heathen at heart and deaf to the truth. Must you forever resist the Holy Spirit? That's what your ancestors did, and so do you! Name one prophet your ancestors didn't persecute! They even killed the ones who predicted the coming of the Righteous One—the Messiah whom you betrayed and murdered. You deliberately disobeyed God's law, even though you received it from the hands of angels."

The Jewish leaders were infuriated by Stephen's accusation, and they shook their fists at him in rage. But Stephen, full of the Holy Spirit, gazed steadily into heaven and saw the glory of God, and he saw Jesus standing in the place of honor at God's right hand. And he told them, "Look, I see the heavens opened and the Son of Man standing in the place of honor at God's right hand!"

Then they put their hands over their ears and began shouting. They rushed at him and dragged him out of the city and began to stone him. His accusers took off their coats and laid them at the feet of a young man named Saul.

As they stoned him, Stephen prayed, "Lord Jesus, receive my spirit." He fell to his knees, shouting, "Lord, don't charge them with this sin!" And with that, he died.

CHAPTER
EIGHT

Saul was one of the witnesses, and he agreed completely with the killing of Stephen.

Persecution Scatters the Believers

A great wave of persecution began that day, sweeping over the church in Jerusalem; and all the believers except the apostles were scattered through the regions of Judea and Samaria. (Some devout men came and buried Stephen with great mourning.) But Saul was going everywhere to destroy the church. He went from house to house, dragging out both men and women to throw them into prison.

Philip Preaches in Samaria

But the believers who were scattered preached the Good News about Jesus wherever they went. Philip, for example, went to the city of Samaria and told

PHILIP

Philip spread the gospel wherever he went, including
Samaria—the last place many Jews would go due to age-
old prejudice. The Samaritans responded in large numbers. In the middle of all this success and excitement, God
directed Philip out to the desert for an appointment with
an Ethiopian eunuch, another foreigner, who had been
in Jerusalem. Philip went immediately. His effectiveness
in sharing the gospel with this man placed a Christian
of significant position in a distant country and may well
have had an effect on an entire nation. Philip began the
conversion of the Gentiles, which Paul continued across
the entire Roman Empire.

+ **STRENGTHS AND ACCOMPLISHMENTS:** One of the seven orga-
  nizers of food distribution in the early church

  Became an evangelist, one of the first traveling
  missionaries

  One of the first to obey Jesus' command to take the
  gospel to all people

  A careful student of the Bible who could explain its
  meaning clearly

+ **LESSONS FROM HIS LIFE:** God finds great and varied uses
  for those willing to obey wholeheartedly

  The gospel is universal Good News

  The whole Bible, not just the New Testament, helps us
  understand more about Jesus

  Both mass response (the Samaritans) and individual
  response (the man from Ethiopia) to the gospel
  are valuable

+ **VITAL STATISTICS:** Occupations: Organizer of food distribution, evangelist

  Relatives: Four daughters, who had the gift of prophecy

the people there about the Messiah. Crowds listened intently to Philip because they were eager to hear his message and see the miraculous signs he did. Many evil spirits were cast out, screaming as they left their victims. And many who had been paralyzed or lame were healed. So there was great joy in that city.

A man named Simon had been a sorcerer there for many years, amazing the people of Samaria and claiming to be someone great. Everyone, from the least to the greatest, often spoke of him as "the Great One—the Power of God." They listened closely to him because for a long time he had astounded them with his magic.

But now the people believed Philip's message of Good News concerning the Kingdom of God and the name of Jesus Christ. As a result, many men and women were baptized. Then Simon himself believed and was baptized. He began following Philip wherever he went, and he was amazed by the signs and great miracles Philip performed.

When the apostles in Jerusalem heard that the people of Samaria had accepted God's message, they sent Peter and John there. As soon as they arrived, they prayed for these new believers to receive the Holy Spirit. The Holy Spirit had not yet come upon any of them, for they had only been baptized in the name of the Lord Jesus. Then Peter and John laid their hands upon these believers, and they received the Holy Spirit.

When Simon saw that the Spirit was given when the apostles laid their hands on people, he offered them money to buy this power. "Let me have this power, too," he exclaimed, "so that when I lay my hands on people, they will receive the Holy Spirit!"

But Peter replied, "May your money be destroyed with you for thinking God's gift can be bought! You can have no part in this, for your heart is not right with God. Repent of your wickedness and pray to the Lord. Perhaps he will forgive your evil thoughts, for I can see that you are full of bitter jealousy and are held captive by sin."

"Pray to the Lord for me," Simon exclaimed, "that these terrible things you've said won't happen to me!"

After testifying and preaching the word of the Lord in Samaria, Peter and John returned to Jerusalem. And they stopped in many Samaritan villages along the way to preach the Good News.

PHILIP AND THE ETHIOPIAN EUNUCH

As for Philip, an angel of the Lord said to him, "Go south down the desert road that runs from Jerusalem to Gaza." So he started out, and he met the treasurer of Ethiopia, a eunuch of great authority under the Kandake, the queen of Ethiopia. The eunuch had gone to Jerusalem to worship, and he was now returning. Seated in his carriage, he was reading aloud from the book of the prophet Isaiah.

The Holy Spirit said to Philip, "Go over and walk along beside the carriage."

Philip ran over and heard the man reading from the prophet Isaiah. Philip asked, "Do you understand what you are reading?"

The man replied, "How can I, unless someone

instructs me?" And he urged Philip to come up into the carriage and sit with him.

The passage of Scripture he had been reading was this:

> *"He was led like a sheep to the slaughter.*
> *And as a lamb is silent before the shearers,*
> *he did not open his mouth.*
> *He was humiliated and received no justice.*
> *Who can speak of his descendants?*
> *For his life was taken from the earth."*

The eunuch asked Philip, "Tell me, was the prophet talking about himself or someone else?" So beginning with this same Scripture, Philip told him the Good News about Jesus.

As they rode along, they came to some water, and the eunuch said, "Look! There's some water! Why can't I be baptized?" He ordered the carriage to stop, and they went down into the water, and Philip baptized him.

When they came up out of the water, the Spirit of the Lord snatched Philip away. The eunuch never saw him again but went on his way rejoicing. Meanwhile, Philip found himself farther north at the town of Azotus. He preached the Good News there and in every town along the way until he came to Caesarea.

CHAPTER
NINE

Saul's Conversion

Meanwhile, Saul was uttering threats with every breath and was eager to kill the Lord's followers. So he went to the high priest. He requested letters addressed to the synagogues in Damascus, asking for their cooperation in the arrest of any followers of the Way he found there. He wanted to bring them—both men and women—back to Jerusalem in chains.

As he was approaching Damascus on this mission, a light from heaven suddenly shone down around him. He fell to the ground and heard a voice saying to him, "Saul! Saul! Why are you persecuting me?"

"Who are you, lord?" Saul asked.

And the voice replied, "I am Jesus, the one you are persecuting! Now get up and go into the city, and you will be told what you must do."

The men with Saul stood speechless, for they heard the sound of someone's voice but saw no one! Saul picked himself up off the ground, but when he opened his eyes he was blind. So his companions led him by the hand to Damascus. He remained there blind for three days and did not eat or drink.

Now there was a believer in Damascus named Ananias. The Lord spoke to him in a vision, calling, "Ananias!"

"Yes, Lord!" he replied.

The Lord said, "Go over to Straight Street, to the house of Judas. When you get there, ask for a man from Tarsus named Saul. He is praying to me right now. I have shown him a vision of a man named Ananias coming in and laying hands on him so he can see again."

"But Lord," exclaimed Ananias, "I've heard many people talk about the terrible things this man has done to the believers in Jerusalem! And he is authorized by the leading priests to arrest everyone who calls upon your name."

But the Lord said, "Go, for Saul is my chosen instrument to take my message to the Gentiles and to kings, as well as to the people of Israel. And I will show him how much he must suffer for my name's sake."

So Ananias went and found Saul. He laid his hands on him and said, "Brother Saul, the Lord Jesus, who appeared to you on the road, has sent me so that you might regain your sight and be filled with the Holy Spirit." Instantly something like scales fell from Saul's eyes, and he regained his sight.

PAUL

No person, apart from Jesus himself, shaped the history of Christianity like the apostle Paul. After spending much of his effort persecuting Christians, Paul had a personal encounter with Jesus that changed his life. He never lost his fierce intensity, but from then on it was channeled for the gospel.

God did not waste any part of Paul—his background, his training, his citizenship, his mind, or even his weaknesses. Are you willing to let God do the same for you? You will never know all he can do with you until you allow him to have all that you are!

+ **STRENGTHS AND ACCOMPLISHMENTS:** Preached the gospel of Christ throughout the Roman Empire on three missionary journeys

Wrote letters to various churches, which became part of the New Testament

Was never afraid to face an issue head-on and deal with it

Is often called the apostle to the Gentiles

+ **WEAKNESSES AND MISTAKES:** Witnessed and approved of Stephen's stoning

Set out to destroy Christianity by persecuting Christians

+ **LESSONS FROM HIS LIFE:** Obedience results from a relationship with God, but obedience will never create or earn that relationship

Real freedom doesn't come until we no longer have to prove our freedom

God does not waste our time; he will use our past and present circumstances so we may serve him with our futures

+ **VITAL STATISTICS:** Where: Born in Tarsus but became a world traveler for Christ

Occupations: Trained as a Pharisee, learned the tentmaking trade, served as a missionary

Then he got up and was baptized. Afterward he ate some food and regained his strength.

SAUL IN DAMASCUS AND JERUSALEM

Saul stayed with the believers in Damascus for a few days. And immediately he began preaching about Jesus in the synagogues, saying, "He is indeed the Son of God!"

All who heard him were amazed. "Isn't this the same man who caused such devastation among Jesus' followers in Jerusalem?" they asked. "And didn't he come here to arrest them and take them in chains to the leading priests?"

Saul's preaching became more and more powerful, and the Jews in Damascus couldn't refute his proofs that Jesus was indeed the Messiah. After a while some of the Jews plotted together to kill him. They were watching for him day and night at the city gate so they could murder him, but Saul was told about their plot. So during the night, some of the other believers lowered him in a large basket through an opening in the city wall.

When Saul arrived in Jerusalem, he tried to meet with the believers, but they were all afraid of him. They did not believe he had truly become a believer! Then Barnabas brought him to the apostles and told them how Saul had seen the Lord on the way to Damascus and how the Lord had spoken to Saul. He also told them that Saul had preached boldly in the name of Jesus in Damascus.

So Saul stayed with the apostles and went all around Jerusalem with them, preaching boldly in the name of the Lord. He debated with some Greek-speaking Jews, but they tried to murder him. When the believers heard about this, they took him down to Caesarea and sent him away to Tarsus, his hometown.

The church then had peace throughout Judea, Galilee, and Samaria, and it became stronger as the believers lived in the fear of the Lord. And with the encouragement of the Holy Spirit, it also grew in numbers.

Peter Heals Aeneas and Raises Dorcas

Meanwhile, Peter traveled from place to place, and he came down to visit the believers in the town of Lydda. There he met a man named Aeneas, who had been paralyzed and bedridden for eight years. Peter said to him, "Aeneas, Jesus Christ heals you! Get up, and roll up your sleeping mat!" And he was healed instantly. Then the whole population of Lydda and Sharon saw Aeneas walking around, and they turned to the Lord.

There was a believer in Joppa named Tabitha (which in Greek is Dorcas). She was always doing kind things for others and helping the poor. About this time she became ill and died. Her body was washed for burial and laid in an upstairs room. But the believers had heard that Peter was nearby at Lydda, so they sent two men to beg him, "Please come as soon as possible!"

So Peter returned with them; and as soon as he arrived, they took him to the upstairs room. The room was filled with widows who were weeping and showing him the coats and other clothes Dorcas had made for them. But Peter asked them all to leave the room; then he knelt and prayed. Turning to the body he said, "Get up, Tabitha." And she opened her eyes! When she saw Peter, she sat up! He gave her his hand and helped her up. Then he called in the widows and all the believers, and he presented her to them alive.

The news spread through the whole town, and many believed in the Lord. And Peter stayed a long time in Joppa, living with Simon, a tanner of hides.

CHAPTER
TEN

CORNELIUS CALLS FOR PETER

In Caesarea there lived a Roman army officer named Cornelius, who was a captain of the Italian Regiment. He was a devout, God-fearing man, as was everyone in his household. He gave generously to the poor and prayed regularly to God. One afternoon about three o'clock, he had a vision in which he saw an angel of God coming toward him. "Cornelius!" the angel said.

Cornelius stared at him in terror. "What is it, sir?" he asked the angel.

And the angel replied, "Your prayers and gifts to the poor have been received by God as an offering! Now send some men to Joppa, and summon a man named Simon Peter. He is staying with Simon, a tanner who lives near the seashore."

As soon as the angel was gone, Cornelius called

two of his household servants and a devout soldier, one of his personal attendants. He told them what had happened and sent them off to Joppa.

PETER VISITS CORNELIUS

The next day as Cornelius's messengers were nearing the town, Peter went up on the flat roof to pray. It was about noon, and he was hungry. But while a meal was being prepared, he fell into a trance. He saw the sky open, and something like a large sheet was let down by its four corners. In the sheet were all sorts of animals, reptiles, and birds. Then a voice said to him, "Get up, Peter; kill and eat them."

"No, Lord," Peter declared. "I have never eaten anything that our Jewish laws have declared impure and unclean."

But the voice spoke again: "Do not call something unclean if God has made it clean." The same vision was repeated three times. Then the sheet was suddenly pulled up to heaven.

Peter was very perplexed. What could the vision mean? Just then the men sent by Cornelius found Simon's house. Standing outside the gate, they asked if a man named Simon Peter was staying there.

Meanwhile, as Peter was puzzling over the vision, the Holy Spirit said to him, "Three men have come looking for you. Get up, go downstairs, and go with them without hesitation. Don't worry, for I have sent them."

So Peter went down and said, "I'm the man you are looking for. Why have you come?"

They said, "We were sent by Cornelius, a Roman

CORNELIUS

Four significant aspects of Cornelius's character are noted in Acts: (1) he actively sought God, (2) he revered God, (3) he was generous in meeting other people's needs, and (4) he prayed regularly. When Peter shared the gospel with Cornelius and his family, God filled them with his Holy Spirit. They did not adhere to the Jewish cultural laws, but Peter baptized them and welcomed them as equals in the growing Christian church. Another step had been taken in carrying the gospel to the whole world.

Cornelius is an example of God's willingness to use extraordinary means to reach those who desire to know him. He does not play favorites, and he does not hide from those who want to find him. God sent his Son because he loves the whole world—and that includes Peter, Cornelius, and you.

+ **STRENGTHS AND ACCOMPLISHMENTS:** Well respected by the Jews even though he was an officer in the occupying army

Responded to God and encouraged his family to do the same

Helped the young church to realize that the Good News is for all people, both Jews and Gentiles

+ **LESSONS FROM HIS LIFE:** God reaches those who want to know him

The gospel is for all people

When we are willing to seek the truth and be obedient to the light God gives us, God will reward us richly

+ **VITAL STATISTICS:** Where: Caesarea

Occupation: Roman army officer

officer. He is a devout and God-fearing man, well respected by all the Jews. A holy angel instructed him to summon you to his house so that he can hear your message." So Peter invited the men to stay for the night. The next day he went with them, accompanied by some of the brothers from Joppa.

They arrived in Caesarea the following day. Cornelius was waiting for them and had called together his relatives and close friends. As Peter entered his home, Cornelius fell at his feet and worshiped him. But Peter pulled him up and said, "Stand up! I'm a human being just like you!" So they talked together and went inside, where many others were assembled.

Peter told them, "You know it is against our laws for a Jewish man to enter a Gentile home like this or to associate with you. But God has shown me that I should no longer think of anyone as impure or unclean. So I came without objection as soon as I was sent for. Now tell me why you sent for me."

Cornelius replied, "Four days ago I was praying in my house about this same time, three o'clock in the afternoon. Suddenly, a man in dazzling clothes was standing in front of me. He told me, 'Cornelius, your prayer has been heard, and your gifts to the poor have been noticed by God! Now send messengers to Joppa, and summon a man named Simon Peter. He is staying in the home of Simon, a tanner who lives near the seashore.' So I sent for you at once, and it was good of you to come. Now we are all here, waiting before God to hear the message the Lord has given you."

The Gentiles Hear the Good News

Then Peter replied, "I see very clearly that God shows no favoritism. In every nation he accepts those who fear him and do what is right. This is the message of Good News for the people of Israel—that there is peace with God through Jesus Christ, who is Lord of all. You know what happened throughout Judea, beginning in Galilee, after John began preaching his message of baptism. And you know that God anointed Jesus of Nazareth with the Holy Spirit and with power. Then Jesus went around doing good and healing all who were oppressed by the devil, for God was with him.

"And we apostles are witnesses of all he did throughout Judea and in Jerusalem. They put him to death by hanging him on a cross, but God raised him to life on the third day. Then God allowed him to appear, not to the general public, but to us whom God had chosen in advance to be his witnesses. We were those who ate and drank with him after he rose from the dead. And he ordered us to preach everywhere and to testify that Jesus is the one appointed by God to be the judge of all—the living and the dead. He is the one all the prophets testified about, saying that everyone who believes in him will have their sins forgiven through his name."

The Gentiles Receive the Holy Spirit

Even as Peter was saying these things, the Holy Spirit fell upon all who were listening to the message. The Jewish believers who came with Peter were amazed that the gift of the Holy Spirit had been poured out on the Gentiles, too. For they heard them speaking in other tongues and praising God.

Then Peter asked, "Can anyone object to their being baptized, now that they have received the Holy Spirit just as we did?" So he gave orders for them to be baptized in the name of Jesus Christ. Afterward Cornelius asked him to stay with them for several days.

CHAPTER
ELEVEN

Peter Explains His Actions

Soon the news reached the apostles and other believers in Judea that the Gentiles had received the word of God. But when Peter arrived back in Jerusalem, the Jewish believers criticized him. "You entered the home of Gentiles and even ate with them!" they said.

Then Peter told them exactly what had happened. "I was in the town of Joppa," he said, "and while I was praying, I went into a trance and saw a vision. Something like a large sheet was let down by its four corners from the sky. And it came right down to me. When I looked inside the sheet, I saw all sorts of tame and wild animals, reptiles, and birds. And I heard a voice say, 'Get up, Peter; kill and eat them.'

"'No, Lord,' I replied. 'I have never eaten anything that our Jewish laws have declared impure or unclean.'

"But the voice from heaven spoke again: 'Do not call something unclean if God has made it clean.' This happened three times before the sheet and all it contained was pulled back up to heaven.

"Just then three men who had been sent from Caesarea arrived at the house where we were staying. The Holy Spirit told me to go with them and not to worry that they were Gentiles. These six brothers here accompanied me, and we soon entered the home of the man who had sent for us. He told us how an angel had appeared to him in his home and had told him, 'Send messengers to Joppa, and summon a man named Simon Peter. He will tell you how you and everyone in your household can be saved!'

"As I began to speak," Peter continued, "the Holy Spirit fell on them, just as he fell on us at the beginning. Then I thought of the Lord's words when he said, 'John baptized with water, but you will be baptized with the Holy Spirit.' And since God gave these Gentiles the same gift he gave us when we believed in the Lord Jesus Christ, who was I to stand in God's way?"

When the others heard this, they stopped objecting and began praising God. They said, "We can see that God has also given the Gentiles the privilege of repenting of their sins and receiving eternal life."

The Church in Antioch of Syria

Meanwhile, the believers who had been scattered during the persecution after Stephen's death traveled as far as Phoenicia, Cyprus, and Antioch of Syria. They preached the word of God, but only to Jews. However, some of the believers who went to Antioch from Cyprus and Cyrene began preaching to the Gentiles about the Lord Jesus. The power of the Lord was with them, and a large number of these Gentiles believed and turned to the Lord.

When the church at Jerusalem heard what had happened, they sent Barnabas to Antioch. When he arrived and saw this evidence of God's blessing, he was filled with joy, and he encouraged the believers to stay true to the Lord. Barnabas was a good man, full of the Holy Spirit and strong in faith. And many people were brought to the Lord.

Then Barnabas went on to Tarsus to look for Saul. When he found him, he brought him back to Antioch. Both of them stayed there with the church for a full year, teaching large crowds of people. (It was at Antioch that the believers were first called Christians.)

During this time some prophets traveled from Jerusalem to Antioch. One of them named Agabus stood up in one of the meetings and predicted by the Spirit that a great famine was coming upon the entire Roman world. (This was fulfilled during the reign of Claudius.) So the believers in Antioch decided to send relief to the brothers and sisters in Judea, everyone giving as much as they could. This they did, entrusting their gifts to Barnabas and Saul to take to the elders of the church in Jerusalem.

CHAPTER
TWELVE

James Is Killed and Peter Is Imprisoned

About that time King Herod Agrippa began to persecute some believers in the church. He had the apostle James (John's brother) killed with a sword. When Herod saw how much this pleased the Jewish people, he also arrested Peter. (This took place during the Passover celebration.) Then he imprisoned him, placing him under the guard of four squads of four soldiers each. Herod intended to bring Peter out for public trial after the Passover. But while Peter was in prison, the church prayed very earnestly for him.

Peter's Miraculous Escape from Prison

The night before Peter was to be placed on trial, he was asleep, fastened with two chains between two soldiers. Others stood guard at the prison gate.

Jesus' mother, Mary, at the foot of the cross

"Father, forgive them, for they don't know what they are doing." —Jesus
LUKE 23:34

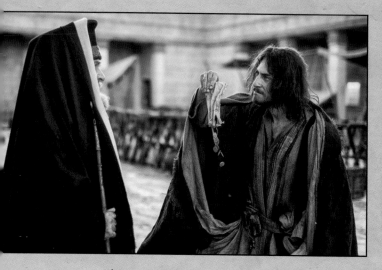

"I have betrayed an innocent man."
— Judas
MATTHEW 27:4

[Joseph] took Jesus' body down from the cross...and laid it in a tomb that had been carved out of the rock. MARK 15:46

Mary Magdalene finds Jesus' tomb empty

They found that the stone had been rolled away. LUKE 24:2

Jesus appears to the disciples in the upper room

Peter fishing on the Sea
of Galilee

At dawn Jesus was standing on the beach.
JOHN 21:4

Peter swims to shore to meet Jesus

On the day of Pentecost all the believers
were meeting together.
ACTS 2:1

Pilate and Claudia

Antipas and
Herodias

Peter and John

Cornelius and the Roman guards

John is beaten and imprisoned

Peter before the Sanhedrin

Saul examining Stephen after his stoning

As they stoned him, Stephen prayed, "Lord Jesus, receive my spirit."
ACTS 7:59

Saul hunting for Christians

HEROD AGRIPPA I

Herod Agrippa I had a Jewish grandmother of royal blood (Mariamne), which allowed the people to accept him—though grudgingly. But soon Herod made a fatal error. During a visit to Caesarea, the people called him a god, and he accepted their praise. Herod was immediately struck with a painful disease, and he died within a week.

Herod Agrippa I had no reverence and no qualms about taking praise that only God should receive. His mistake is a common one. Whenever we become proud of our own abilities and accomplishments, not recognizing them as gifts from God, we repeat Herod's sin.

+ **STRENGTHS AND ACCOMPLISHMENTS**: Capable administrator and negotiator

Managed to maintain good relations with the Jews in his region and with Rome

+ **WEAKNESSES AND MISTAKES**: Arranged the murder of the apostle James

Imprisoned Peter with plans to execute him

Allowed the people to praise him as a god

+ **LESSONS FROM HIS LIFE**: Those who set themselves against God are doomed to ultimate failure

Family traits can influence children toward great good or great evil

+ **VITAL STATISTICS**: Where: Jerusalem

Occupation: Roman-appointed king of the Jews

Relatives: Grandfather: Herod the Great. Father: Aristobulus. Uncle: Herod Antipas. Sister: Herodias. Wife: Cypros. Son: Herod Agrippa II. Daughters: Bernice, Mariamne, Drusilla.

Suddenly, there was a bright light in the cell, and an angel of the Lord stood before Peter. The angel struck him on the side to awaken him and said, "Quick! Get up!" And the chains fell off his wrists. Then the angel told him, "Get dressed and put on your sandals." And he did. "Now put on your coat and follow me," the angel ordered.

So Peter left the cell, following the angel. But all the time he thought it was a vision. He didn't realize it was actually happening. They passed the first and second guard posts and came to the iron gate leading to the city, and this opened for them all by itself. So they passed through and started walking down the street, and then the angel suddenly left him.

Peter finally came to his senses. "It's really true!" he said. "The Lord has sent his angel and saved me from Herod and from what the Jewish leaders had planned to do to me!"

When he realized this, he went to the home of Mary, the mother of John Mark, where many were gathered for prayer. He knocked at the door in the gate, and a servant girl named Rhoda came to open it. When she recognized Peter's voice, she was so overjoyed that, instead of opening the door, she ran back inside and told everyone, "Peter is standing at the door!"

"You're out of your mind!" they said. When she insisted, they decided, "It must be his angel."

Meanwhile, Peter continued knocking. When they finally opened the door and saw him, they were amazed. He motioned for them to quiet down and told them how the Lord had led him out of prison.

JOHN MARK

John Mark was eager to do the right thing, but he had trouble staying with a task. In his Gospel, Mark mentions a young man (probably referring to himself) who fled in such fear during Jesus' arrest that he left his clothes behind. This tendency to run showed up later when Paul and Barnabas took him as their assistant on their first missionary journey. At their second stop, Mark left them and returned to Jerusalem. But Barnabas was patient with Mark, and Mark became a valuable companion to three early Christian leaders: Barnabas, Paul, and Peter.

Mark's role as an assistant allowed him to be an observer. He heard Peter's accounts of the years with Jesus over and over, and he was one of the first to put Jesus' life in writing. Mark's life challenges us to learn from our mistakes and appreciate the patience of others.

+ **STRENGTHS AND ACCOMPLISHMENTS:** Wrote the Gospel of Mark

Provided his family's home as one of the main meeting places for the Christians in Jerusalem

Was a traveling companion to three of the greatest early missionaries

+ **WEAKNESSES AND MISTAKES:** Fled in panic when Jesus was arrested

Left Paul and Barnabas for unknown reasons during their first missionary journey

+ **LESSONS FROM HIS LIFE:** Mistakes are not usually as important as what can be learned from them

Encouragement can change a person's life

+ **VITAL STATISTICS:** Where: Jerusalem

Occupations: Missionary-in-training, Gospel writer, traveling companion

Relatives: Mother: Mary. Cousin: Barnabas.

"Tell James and the other brothers what happened," he said. And then he went to another place.

At dawn there was a great commotion among the soldiers about what had happened to Peter. Herod Agrippa ordered a thorough search for him. When he couldn't be found, Herod interrogated the guards and sentenced them to death. Afterward Herod left Judea to stay in Caesarea for a while.

THE DEATH OF HEROD AGRIPPA

Now Herod was very angry with the people of Tyre and Sidon. So they sent a delegation to make peace with him because their cities were dependent upon Herod's country for food. The delegates won the support of Blastus, Herod's personal assistant, and an appointment with Herod was granted. When the day arrived, Herod put on his royal robes, sat on his throne, and made a speech to them. The people gave him a great ovation, shouting, "It's the voice of a god, not of a man!"

Instantly, an angel of the Lord struck Herod with a sickness, because he accepted the people's worship instead of giving the glory to God. So he was consumed with worms and died.

Meanwhile, the word of God continued to spread, and there were many new believers.

When Barnabas and Saul had finished their mission to Jerusalem, they returned, taking John Mark with them.

CHAPTER
THIRTEEN

Barnabas and Saul Are Commissioned

Among the prophets and teachers of the church at Antioch of Syria were Barnabas, Simeon (called "the black man"), Lucius (from Cyrene), Manaen (the childhood companion of King Herod Antipas), and Saul. One day as these men were worshiping the Lord and fasting, the Holy Spirit said, "Dedicate Barnabas and Saul for the special work to which I have called them." So after more fasting and prayer, the men laid their hands on them and sent them on their way.

Paul's First Missionary Journey

So Barnabas and Saul were sent out by the Holy Spirit. They went down to the seaport of Seleucia and then sailed for the island of Cyprus. There, in the town of Salamis, they went to the Jewish synagogues and preached the word of God. John Mark went with them as their assistant.

Afterward they traveled from town to town across the entire island until finally they reached Paphos, where they met a Jewish sorcerer, a false prophet named Bar-Jesus. He had attached himself to the governor, Sergius Paulus, who was an intelligent man. The governor invited Barnabas and Saul to visit him, for he wanted to hear the word of God. But Elymas, the sorcerer (as his name means in Greek), interfered and urged the governor to pay no attention to what Barnabas and Saul said. He was trying to keep the governor from believing.

Saul, also known as Paul, was filled with the Holy Spirit, and he looked the sorcerer in the eye. Then he said, "You son of the devil, full of every sort of deceit and fraud, and enemy of all that is good! Will you never stop perverting the true ways of the Lord? Watch now, for the Lord has laid his hand of punishment upon you, and you will be struck blind. You will not see the sunlight for some time." Instantly mist and darkness came over the man's eyes, and he began groping around begging for someone to take his hand and lead him.

When the governor saw what had happened, he became a believer, for he was astonished at the teaching about the Lord.

PAUL PREACHES IN ANTIOCH OF PISIDIA

Paul and his companions then left Paphos by ship for Pamphylia, landing at the port town of Perga. There John Mark left them and returned to Jerusalem. But

Paul and Barnabas traveled inland to Antioch of Pisidia.

On the Sabbath they went to the synagogue for the services. After the usual readings from the books of Moses and the prophets, those in charge of the service sent them this message: "Brothers, if you have any word of encouragement for the people, come and give it."

So Paul stood, lifted his hand to quiet them, and started speaking. "Men of Israel," he said, "and you God-fearing Gentiles, listen to me.

"The God of this nation of Israel chose our ancestors and made them multiply and grow strong during their stay in Egypt. Then with a powerful arm he led them out of their slavery. He put up with them through forty years of wandering in the wilderness. Then he destroyed seven nations in Canaan and gave their land to Israel as an inheritance. All this took about 450 years.

"After that, God gave them judges to rule until the time of Samuel the prophet. Then the people begged for a king, and God gave them Saul son of Kish, a man of the tribe of Benjamin, who reigned for forty years. But God removed Saul and replaced him with David, a man about whom God said, 'I have found David son of Jesse, a man after my own heart. He will do everything I want him to do.'

"And it is one of King David's descendants, Jesus, who is God's promised Savior of Israel! Before he came, John the Baptist preached that all the people of Israel needed to repent of their sins and turn to God and be baptized. As John was finishing his ministry he asked, 'Do you think I am the Messiah? No, I am not! But he is coming soon—and I'm not even worthy to be his slave and untie the sandals on his feet.'

"Brothers—you sons of Abraham, and also you God-fearing Gentiles—this message of salvation has been sent to us! The people in Jerusalem and their leaders did not recognize Jesus as the one the prophets had spoken about. Instead, they condemned him, and in doing this they fulfilled the prophets' words that are read every Sabbath. They found no legal reason to execute him, but they asked Pilate to have him killed anyway.

"When they had done all that the prophecies said about him, they took him down from the cross and placed him in a tomb. But God raised him from the dead! And over a period of many days he appeared to those who had gone with him from Galilee to Jerusalem. They are now his witnesses to the people of Israel.

"And now we are here to bring you this Good News. The promise was made to our ancestors, and God has now fulfilled it for us, their descendants, by raising Jesus. This is what the second psalm says about Jesus:

'You are my Son.
    Today I have become your Father.'

For God had promised to raise him from the dead, not leaving him to rot in the grave. He said, 'I will give you the sacred blessings I promised to David.' Another psalm explains it more fully: 'You will not allow your Holy One to rot in the grave.' This is not a reference to David, for after David had done the will of God in his own generation, he died and was buried with his ancestors, and his body decayed. No, it was a reference to someone else—someone whom God raised and whose body did not decay.

"Brothers, listen! We are here to proclaim that through this man Jesus there is forgiveness for your sins. Everyone who believes in him is declared right with God—something the law of Moses could never do. Be careful! Don't let the prophets' words apply to you. For they said,

> 'Look, you mockers,
>   be amazed and die!
> For I am doing something in your own day,
>   something you wouldn't believe
>   even if someone told you about it.'"

As Paul and Barnabas left the synagogue that day, the people begged them to speak about these things again the next week. Many Jews and devout converts to Judaism followed Paul and Barnabas, and the two men urged them to continue to rely on the grace of God.

PAUL TURNS TO THE GENTILES

The following week almost the entire city turned out to hear them preach the word of the Lord. But when some of the Jews saw the crowds, they were jealous; so they slandered Paul and argued against whatever he said.

Then Paul and Barnabas spoke out boldly and declared, "It was necessary that we first preach the word of God to you Jews. But since you have rejected it and judged yourselves unworthy of eternal life, we will offer it to the Gentiles. For the Lord gave us this command when he said,

> *'I have made you a light to the Gentiles,*
> *   to bring salvation to the farthest corners of the*
> * earth.'"*

When the Gentiles heard this, they were very glad and thanked the Lord for his message; and all who were chosen for eternal life became believers. So the Lord's message spread throughout that region.

Then the Jews stirred up the influential religious women and the leaders of the city, and they incited a mob against Paul and Barnabas and ran them out of town. So they shook the dust from their feet as a sign of rejection and went to the town of Iconium. And the believers were filled with joy and with the Holy Spirit.

BARNABAS

Originally named Joseph, this man was such an encourager that he earned the nickname "Son of Encouragement," or Barnabas, from the Jerusalem Christians. Barnabas's actions were crucial to the early church. God used his relationship with Paul at one point and with Mark at another to keep these two men going when either might have failed.

As Barnabas's life shows, we are often presented with situations where someone needs encouragement. Our tendency, however, is to criticize instead. It may be important at times to point out someone's shortcomings in an effort to spur growth, but before we have the right to do this, we must build that person's trust through encouragement. Will you take the opportunity to encourage those with whom you come in contact today?

+ STRENGTHS AND ACCOMPLISHMENTS: One of the first to sell possessions to help the Christians in Jerusalem

First to travel with Paul as a missionary team

Was an encourager, as his nickname shows, and thus one of the most quietly influential people in the early days of Christianity

Called an apostle, although not one of the original Twelve

+ WEAKNESS AND MISTAKE: Like Peter, temporarily stayed aloof from Gentile believers until Paul corrected him

+ LESSONS FROM HIS LIFE: Encouragement is one of the most effective ways to help others

Sooner or later, true obedience to God will involve risk

There is always someone who needs encouragement

+ VITAL STATISTICS: Where: Cyprus, Jerusalem, Antioch

Occupations: Missionary, teacher

Relatives: Aunt: Mary. Cousin: John Mark.

CHAPTER

FOURTEEN

Paul and Barnabas in Iconium

The same thing happened in Iconium. Paul and Barnabas went to the Jewish synagogue and preached
with such power that a great number of both Jews
and Greeks became believers. Some of the Jews, however, spurned God's message and poisoned the minds
of the Gentiles against Paul and Barnabas. But the
apostles stayed there a long time, preaching boldly
about the grace of the Lord. And the Lord proved
their message was true by giving them power to do
miraculous signs and wonders. But the people of the
town were divided in their opinion about them. Some
sided with the Jews, and some with the apostles.

Then a mob of Gentiles and Jews, along with
their leaders, decided to attack and stone them.
When the apostles learned of it, they fled to the
region of Lycaonia—to the towns of Lystra and

Derbe and the surrounding area. And there they preached the Good News.

PAUL AND BARNABAS IN LYSTRA AND DERBE

While they were at Lystra, Paul and Barnabas came upon a man with crippled feet. He had been that way from birth, so he had never walked. He was sitting and listening as Paul preached. Looking straight at him, Paul realized he had faith to be healed. So Paul called to him in a loud voice, "Stand up!" And the man jumped to his feet and started walking.

When the crowd saw what Paul had done, they shouted in their local dialect, "These men are gods in human form!" They decided that Barnabas was the Greek god Zeus and that Paul was Hermes, since he was the chief speaker. Now the temple of Zeus was located just outside the town. So the priest of the temple and the crowd brought bulls and wreaths of flowers to the town gates, and they prepared to offer sacrifices to the apostles.

But when the apostles Barnabas and Paul heard what was happening, they tore their clothing in dismay and ran out among the people, shouting, "Friends, why are you doing this? We are merely human beings—just like you! We have come to bring you the Good News that you should turn from these worthless things and turn to the living God, who made heaven and earth, the sea, and everything in them. In the past he permitted all the nations to go their own ways, but he never left them without evidence of himself and his goodness. For instance, he sends you rain and good crops and gives you food and joyful hearts." But even with these words, Paul and Barnabas could scarcely restrain the people from sacrificing to them.

Then some Jews arrived from Antioch and Iconium and won the crowds to their side. They stoned Paul and dragged him out of town, thinking he was dead. But as the believers gathered around him, he got up and went back into the town. The next day he left with Barnabas for Derbe.

PAUL AND BARNABAS RETURN TO ANTIOCH OF SYRIA

After preaching the Good News in Derbe and making many disciples, Paul and Barnabas returned to Lystra, Iconium, and Antioch of Pisidia, where they strengthened the believers. They encouraged them to continue in the faith, reminding them that we must suffer many hardships to enter the Kingdom of God. Paul and Barnabas also appointed elders in every church. With prayer and fasting, they turned the elders over to the care of the Lord, in whom they had put their trust. Then they traveled back through Pisidia to Pamphylia. They preached the word in Perga, then went down to Attalia.

Finally, they returned by ship to Antioch of Syria, where their journey had begun. The believers there had entrusted them to the grace of God to do the work they had now completed. Upon arriving in Antioch, they called the church together and reported everything God had done through them and how he had opened the door of faith to the Gentiles, too. And they stayed there with the believers for a long time.

CHAPTER
FIFTEEN

The Council at Jerusalem

While Paul and Barnabas were at Antioch of Syria, some men from Judea arrived and began to teach the believers: "Unless you are circumcised as required by the law of Moses, you cannot be saved." Paul and Barnabas disagreed with them, arguing vehemently. Finally, the church decided to send Paul and Barnabas to Jerusalem, accompanied by some local believers, to talk to the apostles and elders about this question. The church sent the delegates to Jerusalem, and they stopped along the way in Phoenicia and Samaria to visit the believers. They told them—much to everyone's joy—that the Gentiles, too, were being converted.

When they arrived in Jerusalem, Barnabas and Paul were welcomed by the whole church, including the apostles and elders. They reported everything

God had done through them. But then some of the believers who belonged to the sect of the Pharisees stood up and insisted, "The Gentile converts must be circumcised and required to follow the law of Moses."

So the apostles and elders met together to resolve this issue. At the meeting, after a long discussion, Peter stood and addressed them as follows: "Brothers, you all know that God chose me from among you some time ago to preach to the Gentiles so that they could hear the Good News and believe. God knows people's hearts, and he confirmed that he accepts Gentiles by giving them the Holy Spirit, just as he did to us. He made no distinction between us and them, for he cleansed their hearts through faith. So why are you now challenging God by burdening the Gentile believers with a yoke that neither we nor our ancestors were able to bear? We believe that we are all saved the same way, by the undeserved grace of the Lord Jesus."

Everyone listened quietly as Barnabas and Paul told about the miraculous signs and wonders God had done through them among the Gentiles.

When they had finished, James stood and said, "Brothers, listen to me. Peter has told you about the time God first visited the Gentiles to take from them a people for himself. And this conversion of Gentiles is exactly what the prophets predicted. As it is written:

> *'Afterward I will return*
> *and restore the fallen house of David.*

SILAS

Silas was one of the representatives from Jerusalem sent with Paul and Barnabas to Antioch with an official letter of welcome and acceptance for the Gentile Christians. Having fulfilled this mission, Silas returned to Jerusalem. Within a short time, however, he was back in Antioch at Paul's request to join him on his second missionary journey.

Paul, Silas, and Timothy began a far-ranging ministry that included some exciting adventures. Paul and Silas spent a night singing in a Philippian jail after being severely beaten. An earthquake, the loosing of their chains, and the resulting panic led to the conversion of their jailer and his family. Later, they narrowly missed another beating in Thessalonica, prevented by an evening escape. In Berea there was more trouble, but Silas and Timothy stayed there to teach the young believers.

Silas took advantage of opportunities to serve God and was not discouraged by the setbacks and opposition he met along the way. Though not the most famous of the early missionaries, he was certainly a hero worth imitating.

+ STRENGTHS AND ACCOMPLISHMENTS: A leader in the Jerusalem church

    Was closely associated with Paul from the second missionary journey on

    Worked as a writing secretary for both Paul and Peter

+ LESSONS FROM HIS LIFE: Partnership is a significant part of effective ministry

    Obedience to God will often mean giving up what makes us feel secure

+ VITAL STATISTICS: Where: Roman citizen living in Jerusalem

    Occupation: One of the first career missionaries

I will rebuild its ruins
    and restore it,
so that the rest of humanity might seek
        the LORD,
    including the Gentiles—
    all those I have called to be mine.
The LORD has spoken—
    he who made these things known
        so long ago.'

"And so my judgment is that we should not make it difficult for the Gentiles who are turning to God. Instead, we should write and tell them to abstain from eating food offered to idols, from sexual immorality, from eating the meat of strangled animals, and from consuming blood. For these laws of Moses have been preached in Jewish synagogues in every city on every Sabbath for many generations."

THE LETTER FOR GENTILE BELIEVERS

Then the apostles and elders together with the whole church in Jerusalem chose delegates, and they sent them to Antioch of Syria with Paul and Barnabas to report on this decision. The men chosen were two of the church leaders—Judas (also called Barsabbas) and Silas. This is the letter they took with them:

"This letter is from the apostles and elders, your brothers in Jerusalem. It is written to the Gentile believers in Antioch, Syria, and Cilicia. Greetings!

"We understand that some men from here have troubled you and upset you with their teaching, but we did not send them! So we decided, having come to complete agreement, to send you official representatives, along with our beloved Barnabas and Paul, who have risked their lives for the name of our Lord Jesus Christ. We are sending Judas and Silas to confirm what we have decided concerning your question.

"For it seemed good to the Holy Spirit and to us to lay no greater burden on you than these few requirements: You must abstain from eating food offered to idols, from consuming blood or the meat of strangled animals, and from sexual immorality. If you do this, you will do well. Farewell."

The messengers went at once to Antioch, where they called a general meeting of the believers and delivered the letter. And there was great joy throughout the church that day as they read this encouraging message.

Then Judas and Silas, both being prophets, spoke at length to the believers, encouraging and strengthening their faith. They stayed for a while, and then the believers sent them back to the church in Jerusalem with a blessing of peace. Paul and Barnabas stayed in Antioch. They and many others taught and preached the word of the Lord there.

Paul and Barnabas Separate

After some time Paul said to Barnabas, "Let's go back and visit each city where we previously preached the word of the Lord, to see how the new believers are doing." Barnabas agreed and wanted to take along John Mark. But Paul disagreed strongly, since John Mark had deserted them in Pamphylia and had not continued with them in their work. Their disagreement was so sharp that they separated. Barnabas took John Mark with him and sailed for Cyprus. Paul chose Silas, and as he left, the believers entrusted him to the Lord's gracious care. Then he traveled throughout Syria and Cilicia, strengthening the churches there.

CHAPTER
SIXTEEN

Paul's Second Missionary Journey

Paul went first to Derbe and then to Lystra, where there was a young disciple named Timothy. His mother was a Jewish believer, but his father was a Greek. Timothy was well thought of by the believers in Lystra and Iconium, so Paul wanted him to join them on their journey. In deference to the Jews of the area, he arranged for Timothy to be circumcised before they left, for everyone knew that his father was a Greek. Then they went from town to town, instructing the believers to follow the decisions made by the apostles and elders in Jerusalem. So the churches were strengthened in their faith and grew larger every day.

A Call from Macedonia

Next Paul and Silas traveled through the area of Phrygia and Galatia, because the Holy Spirit had prevented them from preaching the word in the province of Asia at that time. Then coming to the borders of Mysia, they headed north for the province of Bithynia, but again the Spirit of Jesus did not allow them to go there. So instead, they went on through Mysia to the seaport of Troas.

That night Paul had a vision: A man from Macedonia in northern Greece was standing there, pleading with him, "Come over to Macedonia and help us!" So we decided to leave for Macedonia at once, having concluded that God was calling us to preach the Good News there.

Lydia of Philippi Believes in Jesus

We boarded a boat at Troas and sailed straight across to the island of Samothrace, and the next day we landed at Neapolis. From there we reached Philippi, a major city of that district of Macedonia and a Roman colony. And we stayed there several days.

On the Sabbath we went a little way outside the city to a riverbank, where we thought people would be meeting for prayer, and we sat down to speak with some women who had gathered there. One of them was Lydia from Thyatira, a merchant of expensive purple cloth, who worshiped God. As she listened to us, the Lord opened her heart, and she accepted what Paul was saying. She and her household were baptized, and she asked us to be her guests. "If you agree that I am a true believer in the Lord," she said, "come and stay at my home." And she urged us until we agreed.

TIMOTHY

Timothy probably became a Christian after Paul's first missionary visit to Lystra (Acts 16:1-5). Timothy already had solid Jewish training in the Scriptures from his mother and grandmother. By Paul's second visit, Timothy had grown into a respected disciple of Jesus. He did not hesitate to join Paul and Silas on their journey.

Timothy seemed to struggle with a naturally timid character and a sensitivity about his youthfulness. But by God's grace, Paul saw great potential in Timothy. Paul demonstrated his confidence in Timothy by entrusting him with important responsibilities. Paul sent Timothy as his personal representative to Corinth during a particularly tense time (1 Corinthians 4:14-17).

Our last pictures of Timothy come from the most personal letters in the New Testament: 1 and 2 Timothy. Paul wrote to encourage Timothy and give him much-needed direction. These letters have provided comfort and help to countless other "Timothys" throughout the years.

+ **STRENGTHS AND ACCOMPLISHMENTS:** Joined Paul for his second and third missionary journeys

Was a respected Christian in his hometown

Was Paul's special representative on several occasions

Probably knew Paul better than any other person, becoming like a son to Paul

+ **WEAKNESSES AND MISTAKES:** Struggled with a timid and reserved nature

Allowed others to look down on his youthfulness

+ **LESSONS FROM HIS LIFE:** Youthfulness should not be an excuse for ineffectiveness

Our inadequacies and inabilities should not keep us from being available to God

+ **VITAL STATISTICS:** Where: Lystra

Occupations: Missionary, pastor

Relatives: Mother: Eunice. Grandmother: Lois. Father: a Greek.

Paul and Silas in Prison

One day as we were going down to the place of prayer, we met a slave girl who had a spirit that enabled her to tell the future. She earned a lot of money for her masters by telling fortunes. She followed Paul and the rest of us, shouting, "These men are servants of the Most High God, and they have come to tell you how to be saved."

This went on day after day until Paul got so exasperated that he turned and said to the demon within her, "I command you in the name of Jesus Christ to come out of her." And instantly it left her.

Her masters' hopes of wealth were now shattered, so they grabbed Paul and Silas and dragged them before the authorities at the marketplace. "The whole city is in an uproar because of these Jews!" they shouted to the city officials. "They are teaching customs that are illegal for us Romans to practice."

A mob quickly formed against Paul and Silas, and the city officials ordered them stripped and beaten with wooden rods. They were severely beaten, and then they were thrown into prison. The jailer was ordered to make sure they didn't escape. So the jailer put them into the inner dungeon and clamped their feet in the stocks.

Around midnight Paul and Silas were praying and singing hymns to God, and the other prisoners were listening. Suddenly, there was a massive earthquake, and the prison was shaken to its foundations. All the doors immediately flew open, and the chains

LYDIA

Lydia's business as a dealer in fine purple cloth and dye means she was probably wealthy. Lydia was also a spiritual searcher, as she was among the Gentile women who gathered outside Philippi on each Sabbath to pray to the God of the Jews. One eventful day, Paul and Silas visited this group. God responded to her quest by providing her with more truth. When she heard the good news about Jesus Christ, she listened and believed. She is remembered as Paul's first European convert.

Luke described with swift strokes the first two steps in Lydia's life as a disciple: (1) she was baptized, (2) she brought the rest of the members of her household to Paul, and they apparently believed as well, because they were baptized. Lydia's response was both inward and outward. Her life is a reminder that then, as now, the gospel had life-changing effects.

+ **STRENGTHS AND ACCOMPLISHMENTS:** Successful businesswoman

> The first convert to Christianity in Philippi, and therefore, Europe

> Brought her entire household to hear about Jesus, and all were baptized as a result

> Provided housing in Philippi for Paul and Silas

+ **LESSONS FROM HER LIFE:** God rewards those who honestly seek him

> One of the marks of conversion is care for others—physically and spiritually

+ **VITAL STATISTICS:** Where: From Thyatira, living in Philippi

> Occupation: Merchant specializing in costly purple cloth

> Relatives: A household that was baptized with her

of every prisoner fell off! The jailer woke up to see the prison doors wide open. He assumed the prisoners had escaped, so he drew his sword to kill himself. But Paul shouted to him, "Stop! Don't kill yourself! We are all here!"

The jailer called for lights and ran to the dungeon and fell down trembling before Paul and Silas. Then he brought them out and asked, "Sirs, what must I do to be saved?"

They replied, "Believe in the Lord Jesus and you will be saved, along with everyone in your household." And they shared the word of the Lord with him and with all who lived in his household. Even at that hour of the night, the jailer cared for them and washed their wounds. Then he and everyone in his household were immediately baptized. He brought them into his house and set a meal before them, and he and his entire household rejoiced because they all believed in God.

The next morning the city officials sent the police to tell the jailer, "Let those men go!" So the jailer told Paul, "The city officials have said you and Silas are free to leave. Go in peace."

But Paul replied, "They have publicly beaten us without a trial and put us in prison—and we are Roman citizens. So now they want us to leave secretly? Certainly not! Let them come themselves to release us!"

When the police reported this, the city officials were alarmed to learn that Paul and Silas were Roman citizens. So they came to the jail and apologized to them. Then they brought them out and begged them to leave the city. When Paul and Silas left the prison, they returned to the home of Lydia. There they met with the believers and encouraged them once more. Then they left town.

CHAPTER

SEVENTEEN

PAUL PREACHES IN THESSALONICA

Paul and Silas then traveled through the towns of Amphipolis and Apollonia and came to Thessalonica, where there was a Jewish synagogue. As was Paul's custom, he went to the synagogue service, and for three Sabbaths in a row he used the Scriptures to reason with the people. He explained the prophecies and proved that the Messiah must suffer and rise from the dead. He said, "This Jesus I'm telling you about is the Messiah." Some of the Jews who listened were persuaded and joined Paul and Silas, along with many God-fearing Greek men and quite a few prominent women.

But some of the Jews were jealous, so they gathered some troublemakers from the marketplace to form a mob and start a riot. They attacked the home of Jason, searching for Paul and Silas so they could drag them out to the crowd. Not finding them there, they dragged out Jason and some of the other believers instead and took them before the city council. "Paul and Silas have caused trouble all over the world," they shouted, "and now they are here disturbing our city, too. And Jason has welcomed them into his home. They are all guilty of treason against Caesar, for they profess allegiance to another king, named Jesus."

The people of the city, as well as the city council, were thrown into turmoil by these reports. So the officials forced Jason and the other believers to post bond, and then they released them.

PAUL AND SILAS IN BEREA

That very night the believers sent Paul and Silas to Berea. When they arrived there, they went to the Jewish synagogue. And the people of Berea were more open-minded than those in Thessalonica, and they listened eagerly to Paul's message. They searched the Scriptures day after day to see if Paul and Silas were teaching the truth. As a result, many Jews believed, as did many of the prominent Greek women and men.

But when some Jews in Thessalonica learned that Paul was preaching the word of God in Berea, they went there and stirred up trouble. The believers acted at once, sending Paul on to the coast, while Silas and Timothy remained behind. Those escorting Paul went with him all the way to Athens; then they returned to Berea with instructions for Silas and Timothy to hurry and join him.

PAUL PREACHES IN ATHENS

While Paul was waiting for them in Athens, he was deeply troubled by all the idols he saw everywhere in the city. He went to the synagogue to reason with the Jews and the God-fearing Gentiles, and he spoke daily in the public square to all who happened to be there.

He also had a debate with some of the Epicurean and Stoic philosophers. When he told them about Jesus and his resurrection, they said, "What's this babbler trying to say with these strange ideas he's picked up?" Others said, "He seems to be preaching about some foreign gods."

Then they took him to the high council of the city. "Come and tell us about this new teaching," they said. "You are saying some rather strange things, and we want to know what it's all about." (It should be explained that all the Athenians as well as the foreigners in Athens seemed to spend all their time discussing the latest ideas.)

So Paul, standing before the council, addressed them as follows: "Men of Athens, I notice that you are very religious in every way, for as I was walking along I saw your many shrines. And one of your altars had this inscription on it: 'To an Unknown God.' This God, whom you worship without knowing, is the one I'm telling you about.

"He is the God who made the world and everything in it. Since he is Lord of heaven and earth, he doesn't live in man-made temples, and human hands can't serve his needs—for he has no needs.

He himself gives life and breath to everything, and he satisfies every need. From one man he created all the nations throughout the whole earth. He decided beforehand when they should rise and fall, and he determined their boundaries.

"His purpose was for the nations to seek after God and perhaps feel their way toward him and find him—though he is not far from any one of us. For in him we live and move and exist. As some of your own poets have said, 'We are his offspring.' And since this is true, we shouldn't think of God as an idol designed by craftsmen from gold or silver or stone.

"God overlooked people's ignorance about these things in earlier times, but now he commands everyone everywhere to repent of their sins and turn to him. For he has set a day for judging the world with justice by the man he has appointed, and he proved to everyone who this is by raising him from the dead."

When they heard Paul speak about the resurrection of the dead, some laughed in contempt, but others said, "We want to hear more about this later." That ended Paul's discussion with them, but some joined him and became believers. Among them were Dionysius, a member of the council, a woman named Damaris, and others with them.

CHAPTER
EIGHTEEN

Paul Meets Priscilla and Aquila in Corinth

Then Paul left Athens and went to Corinth. There he became acquainted with a Jew named Aquila, born in Pontus, who had recently arrived from Italy with his wife, Priscilla. They had left Italy when Claudius Caesar deported all Jews from Rome. Paul lived and worked with them, for they were tentmakers just as he was.

Each Sabbath found Paul at the synagogue, trying to convince the Jews and Greeks alike. And after Silas and Timothy came down from Macedonia, Paul spent all his time preaching the word. He testified to the Jews that Jesus was the Messiah. But when they opposed and insulted him, Paul shook the dust from his clothes and said, "Your blood is upon your own heads—I am innocent. From now on I will go preach to the Gentiles."

PRISCILLA AND AQUILA

Priscilla and Aquila met Paul in Corinth during his second missionary journey. They had just been expelled from Rome by Emperor Claudius's decree against Jews. Their home was as movable as the tents they made to support themselves. They opened their home to Paul, and he joined them in tentmaking. He shared with them his wealth of spiritual wisdom.

Priscilla and Aquila made the most of their spiritual education. They listened carefully to sermons and evaluated what they heard. When they heard Apollos speak, they realized that his information was not complete. Instead of confronting him openly, the couple quietly took Apollos aside and shared with him what he needed to know.

Back in Rome years later, they hosted one of the house churches that developed. Their hospitality opened the doorway of salvation to many. The Christian home is still one of the best tools for spreading the gospel. Do guests find Christ in your home?

+ **STRENGTHS AND ACCOMPLISHMENTS:** Outstanding husband-and-wife team who ministered in the early church

Supported themselves by tentmaking while serving Christ

Close friends of Paul

Explained to Apollos the full message of Christ

+ **LESSONS FROM THEIR LIVES:** Couples can have an effective ministry together

The home is a valuable tool for evangelism

Every believer needs to be well educated in the faith, whatever his or her role in the church

+ **VITAL STATISTICS:** Where: Originally from Rome, moved to Corinth, then Ephesus

Occupation: Tentmakers

Then he left and went to the home of Titius Justus, a Gentile who worshiped God and lived next door to the synagogue. Crispus, the leader of the synagogue, and everyone in his household believed in the Lord. Many others in Corinth also heard Paul, became believers, and were baptized.

One night the Lord spoke to Paul in a vision and told him, "Don't be afraid! Speak out! Don't be silent! For I am with you, and no one will attack and harm you, for many people in this city belong to me." So Paul stayed there for the next year and a half, teaching the word of God.

But when Gallio became governor of Achaia, some Jews rose up together against Paul and brought him before the governor for judgment. They accused Paul of "persuading people to worship God in ways that are contrary to our law."

But just as Paul started to make his defense, Gallio turned to Paul's accusers and said, "Listen, you Jews, if this were a case involving some wrongdoing or a serious crime, I would have a reason to accept your case. But since it is merely a question of words and names and your Jewish law, take care of it yourselves. I refuse to judge such matters." And he threw them out of the courtroom.

The crowd then grabbed Sosthenes, the leader of the synagogue, and beat him right there in the courtroom. But Gallio paid no attention.

Paul Returns to Antioch of Syria

Paul stayed in Corinth for some time after that, then said good-bye to the brothers and sisters and went to nearby Cenchrea. There he shaved his head according to Jewish custom, marking the end of a vow. Then he set sail for Syria, taking Priscilla and Aquila with him.

They stopped first at the port of Ephesus, where Paul left the others behind. While he was there, he went to the synagogue to reason with the Jews. They asked him to stay longer, but he declined. As he left, however, he said, "I will come back later, God willing." Then he set sail from Ephesus. The next stop was at the port of Caesarea. From there he went up and visited the church at Jerusalem and then went back to Antioch.

After spending some time in Antioch, Paul went back through Galatia and Phrygia, visiting and strengthening all the believers.

APOLLOS INSTRUCTED AT EPHESUS

Meanwhile, a Jew named Apollos, an eloquent speaker who knew the Scriptures well, had arrived in Ephesus from Alexandria in Egypt. He had been taught the way of the Lord, and he taught others about Jesus with an enthusiastic spirit and with accuracy. However, he knew only about John's baptism. When Priscilla and Aquila heard him preaching boldly in the synagogue, they took him aside and explained the way of God even more accurately.

Apollos had been thinking about going to Achaia, and the brothers and sisters in Ephesus encouraged him to go. They wrote to the believers in Achaia, asking them to welcome him. When he arrived there, he proved to be of great benefit to those who, by God's grace, had believed. He refuted the Jews with powerful arguments in public debate. Using the Scriptures, he explained to them that Jesus was the Messiah.

NINETEEN

Paul's Third Missionary Journey

While Apollos was in Corinth, Paul traveled through the interior regions until he reached Ephesus, on the coast, where he found several believers. "Did you receive the Holy Spirit when you believed?" he asked them.

"No," they replied, "we haven't even heard that there is a Holy Spirit."

"Then what baptism did you experience?" he asked.

And they replied, "The baptism of John."

Paul said, "John's baptism called for repentance from sin. But John himself told the people to believe in the one who would come later, meaning Jesus."

As soon as they heard this, they were baptized in the name of the Lord Jesus. Then when Paul laid his hands on them, the Holy Spirit came on them, and they spoke in other tongues and prophesied. There were about twelve men in all.

Paul Ministers in Ephesus

Then Paul went to the synagogue and preached boldly for the next three months, arguing persuasively about the Kingdom of God. But some became stubborn, rejecting his message and publicly speaking against the Way. So Paul left the synagogue and took the believers with him. Then he held daily discussions at the lecture hall of Tyrannus. This went on for the next two years, so that people throughout the province of Asia—both Jews and Greeks—heard the word of the Lord.

God gave Paul the power to perform unusual miracles. When handkerchiefs or aprons that had merely touched his skin were placed on sick people, they were healed of their diseases, and evil spirits were expelled.

A group of Jews was traveling from town to town casting out evil spirits. They tried to use the name of the Lord Jesus in their incantation, saying, "I command you in the name of Jesus, whom Paul preaches, to come out!" Seven sons of Sceva, a leading priest, were doing this. But one time when they tried it, the evil spirit replied, "I know Jesus, and I know Paul, but who are you?" Then the man with the evil spirit leaped on them, overpowered them, and attacked them with such violence that they fled from the house, naked and battered.

The story of what happened spread quickly all through Ephesus, to Jews and Greeks alike.

APOLLOS

When Apollos arrived in Ephesus shortly after Paul's departure, he made an immediate impact. He spoke boldly, interpreting and applying the Old Testament Scriptures effectively. When Priscilla and Aquila heard Apollos speak, they quickly realized that he did not have the whole story. His preaching was based only on the Old Testament and John the Baptist's message. As they told him of Jesus' life, death, and resurrection, and the coming of the Holy Spirit, Apollos was filled with new energy and boldness.

Apollos next decided to travel to Achaia. He quickly became the verbal champion of the Christians in Corinth, publicly debating the opponents of the gospel. Later, when Apollos was preparing to return to Corinth, Paul wrote warmly of Apollos as a fellow minister who had "watered" the seeds of the gospel that Paul had planted in Corinth (1 Corinthians 3:6).

Although his natural abilities could have caused him to be proud, Apollos proved himself willing to learn. Because he did not hesitate to be a student, he became an even better teacher.

+ **STRENGTHS AND ACCOMPLISHMENTS:** A gifted and persuasive preacher and apologist in the early church

  Willing to be taught

+ **LESSONS FROM HIS LIFE:** Effective communication of the gospel includes an accurate message delivered with God's power

  A clear verbal defense of the gospel can be an encouragement to believers, while convincing nonbelievers of its truth

+ **VITAL STATISTICS:** Where: From Alexandria in Egypt

  Occupations: Traveling preacher, apologist

A solemn fear descended on the city, and the name of the Lord Jesus was greatly honored. Many who became believers confessed their sinful practices. A number of them who had been practicing sorcery brought their incantation books and burned them at a public bonfire. The value of the books was several million dollars. So the message about the Lord spread widely and had a powerful effect.

Afterward Paul felt compelled by the Spirit to go over to Macedonia and Achaia before going to Jerusalem. "And after that," he said, "I must go on to Rome!" He sent his two assistants, Timothy and Erastus, ahead to Macedonia while he stayed awhile longer in the province of Asia.

The Riot in Ephesus

About that time, serious trouble developed in Ephesus concerning the Way. It began with Demetrius, a silversmith who had a large business manufacturing silver shrines of the Greek goddess Artemis. He kept many craftsmen busy. He called them together, along with others employed in similar trades, and addressed them as follows:

"Gentlemen, you know that our wealth comes from this business. But as you have seen and heard, this man Paul has persuaded many people that handmade gods aren't really gods at all. And he's done this not only here in Ephesus but throughout the entire province! Of course, I'm not just talking about the loss of public respect for our business. I'm also concerned that the temple of the great goddess Artemis will lose its influence and that Artemis—this magnificent goddess worshiped throughout the province of Asia and all around the world—will be robbed of her great prestige!"

At this their anger boiled, and they began shouting, "Great is Artemis of the Ephesians!" Soon the whole city was filled with confusion. Everyone rushed to the amphitheater, dragging along Gaius and Aristarchus, who were Paul's traveling companions from Macedonia. Paul wanted to go in, too, but the believers wouldn't let him. Some of the officials of the province, friends of Paul, also sent a message to him, begging him not to risk his life by entering the amphitheater.

Inside, the people were all shouting, some one thing and some another. Everything was in confusion. In fact, most of them didn't even know why they were there. The Jews in the crowd pushed Alexander forward and told him to explain the situation. He motioned for silence and tried to speak. But when the crowd realized he was a Jew, they started shouting again and kept it up for about two hours: "Great is Artemis of the Ephesians! Great is Artemis of the Ephesians!"

At last the mayor was able to quiet them down enough to speak. "Citizens of Ephesus," he said. "Everyone knows that Ephesus is the official guardian of the temple of the great Artemis, whose image fell down to us from heaven. Since this is an undeniable fact, you should stay calm and not do anything rash. You have brought these men here, but they have stolen nothing from the temple and have not spoken against our goddess.

"If Demetrius and the craftsmen have a case against them, the courts are in session and the officials can hear the case at once. Let them make formal charges. And if there are complaints about other matters, they can be settled in a legal assembly. I am afraid we are in danger of being charged with rioting by the Roman government, since there is no cause for all this commotion. And if Rome demands an explanation, we won't know what to say." Then he dismissed them, and they dispersed.

CHAPTER

TWENTY

PAUL GOES TO MACEDONIA AND GREECE

When the uproar was over, Paul sent for the believers and encouraged them. Then he said good-bye and left for Macedonia. While there, he encouraged the believers in all the towns he passed through. Then he traveled down to Greece, where he stayed for three months. He was preparing to sail back to Syria when he discovered a plot by some Jews against his life, so he decided to return through Macedonia.

Several men were traveling with him. They were Sopater son of Pyrrhus from Berea; Aristarchus and Secundus from Thessalonica; Gaius from Derbe; Timothy; and Tychicus and Trophimus from the province of Asia. They went on ahead and waited for us at Troas. After the Passover ended, we boarded a ship at Philippi in Macedonia and five days later joined them in Troas, where we stayed a week.

Paul's Final Visit to Troas

On the first day of the week, we gathered with the local believers to share in the Lord's Supper. Paul was preaching to them, and since he was leaving the next day, he kept talking until midnight. The upstairs room where we met was lighted with many flickering lamps. As Paul spoke on and on, a young man named Eutychus, sitting on the windowsill, became very drowsy. Finally, he fell sound asleep and dropped three stories to his death below. Paul went down, bent over him, and took him into his arms. "Don't worry," he said, "he's alive!" Then they all went back upstairs, shared in the Lord's Supper, and ate together. Paul continued talking to them until dawn, and then he left. Meanwhile, the young man was taken home alive and well, and everyone was greatly relieved.

Paul Meets the Ephesian Elders

Paul went by land to Assos, where he had arranged for us to join him, while we traveled by ship. He joined us there, and we sailed together to Mitylene. The next day we sailed past the island of Kios. The following day we crossed to the island of Samos, and a day later we arrived at Miletus.

Paul had decided to sail on past Ephesus, for he didn't want to spend any more time in the province of Asia. He was hurrying to get to Jerusalem, if possible, in time for the Festival of Pentecost. But when we landed at Miletus, he sent a message to the elders of the church at Ephesus, asking them to come and meet him.

When they arrived he declared, "You know that from the day I set foot in the province of Asia until now I have done the Lord's work humbly and with many tears. I have endured the trials that came to me from the plots of the Jews. I never shrank back from telling you what you needed to hear, either publicly or in your homes. I have had one message for Jews and Greeks alike—the necessity of repenting from sin and turning to God, and of having faith in our Lord Jesus.

"And now I am bound by the Spirit to go to Jerusalem. I don't know what awaits me, except that the Holy Spirit tells me in city after city that jail and suffering lie ahead. But my life is worth nothing to me unless I use it for finishing the work assigned me by the Lord Jesus—the work of telling others the Good News about the wonderful grace of God.

"And now I know that none of you to whom I have preached the Kingdom will ever see me again. I declare today that I have been faithful. If anyone suffers eternal death, it's not my fault, for I didn't shrink from declaring all that God wants you to know.

"So guard yourselves and God's people. Feed and shepherd God's flock—his church, purchased with his own blood—over which the Holy Spirit has appointed you as elders. I know that false teachers, like vicious wolves, will come in among you after I leave, not sparing the flock. Even some men from your own group will rise up and distort the truth in order to draw a following. Watch out! Remember the three years I was with you—my constant watch and care over you night and day, and my many tears for you.

"And now I entrust you to God and the message of his grace that is able to build you up and give you an inheritance with all those he has set apart for himself.

"I have never coveted anyone's silver or gold or fine clothes. You know that these hands of mine have worked to supply my own needs and even the needs of those who were with me. And I have been a constant example of how you can help those in need by working hard. You should remember the words of the Lord Jesus: 'It is more blessed to give than to receive.'"

When he had finished speaking, he knelt and prayed with them. They all cried as they embraced and kissed him good-bye. They were sad most of all because he had said that they would never see him again. Then they escorted him down to the ship.

CHAPTER
TWENTY-ONE

Paul's Journey to Jerusalem

After saying farewell to the Ephesian elders, we sailed straight to the island of Cos. The next day we reached Rhodes and then went to Patara. There we boarded a ship sailing for Phoenicia. We sighted the island of Cyprus, passed it on our left, and landed at the harbor of Tyre, in Syria, where the ship was to unload its cargo.

We went ashore, found the local believers, and stayed with them a week. These believers prophesied through the Holy Spirit that Paul should not go on to Jerusalem. When we returned to the ship at the end of the week, the entire congregation, including women and children, left the city and came down to the shore with us. There we knelt, prayed, and said our farewells. Then we went aboard, and they returned home.

The next stop after leaving Tyre was Ptolemais, where we greeted the brothers and sisters and stayed for one day. The next day we went on to Caesarea and stayed at the home of Philip the Evangelist, one of the seven men who had been chosen to distribute food. He had four unmarried daughters who had the gift of prophecy.

Several days later a man named Agabus, who also had the gift of prophecy, arrived from Judea. He came over, took Paul's belt, and bound his own feet and hands with it. Then he said, "The Holy Spirit declares, 'So shall the owner of this belt be bound by the Jewish leaders in Jerusalem and turned over to the Gentiles.'" When we heard this, we and the local believers all begged Paul not to go on to Jerusalem.

But he said, "Why all this weeping? You are breaking my heart! I am ready not only to be jailed at Jerusalem but even to die for the sake of the Lord Jesus." When it was clear that we couldn't persuade him, we gave up and said, "The Lord's will be done."

PAUL ARRIVES AT JERUSALEM

After this we packed our things and left for Jerusalem. Some believers from Caesarea accompanied us, and they took us to the home of Mnason, a man originally from Cyprus and one of the early believers. When we arrived, the brothers and sisters in Jerusalem welcomed us warmly.

The next day Paul went with us to meet with James, and all the elders of the Jerusalem church were present. After greeting them, Paul gave a detailed account of the things God had accomplished among the Gentiles through his ministry.

After hearing this, they praised God. And then they said, "You know, dear brother, how many thousands of Jews have also believed, and they all follow the law of Moses very seriously. But the Jewish believers here in Jerusalem have been told that you are teaching all the Jews who live among the Gentiles to turn their backs on the laws of Moses. They've heard that you teach them not to circumcise their children or follow other Jewish customs. What should we do? They will certainly hear that you have come.

"Here's what we want you to do. We have four men here who have completed their vow. Go with them to the Temple and join them in the purification ceremony, paying for them to have their heads ritually shaved. Then everyone will know that the rumors are all false and that you yourself observe the Jewish laws.

"As for the Gentile believers, they should do what we already told them in a letter: They should abstain from eating food offered to idols, from consuming blood or the meat of strangled animals, and from sexual immorality."

Paul Is Arrested

So Paul went to the Temple the next day with the other men. They had already started the purification ritual, so he publicly announced the date when their vows would end and sacrifices would be offered for each of them.

The seven days were almost ended when some Jews from the province of Asia saw Paul in the Temple and roused a mob against him. They grabbed him, yelling, "Men of Israel, help us! This is the man who preaches against our people everywhere and tells everybody to disobey the Jewish laws. He speaks against the Temple—and even defiles this holy place by bringing in Gentiles." (For earlier that day they had seen him in the city with Trophimus, a Gentile from Ephesus, and they assumed Paul had taken him into the Temple.)

The whole city was rocked by these accusations, and a great riot followed. Paul was grabbed and dragged out of the Temple, and immediately the gates were closed behind him. As they were trying to kill him, word reached the commander of the Roman regiment that all Jerusalem was in an uproar. He immediately called out his soldiers and officers and ran down among the crowd. When the mob saw the commander and the troops coming, they stopped beating Paul.

Then the commander arrested him and ordered him bound with two chains. He asked the crowd who he was and what he had done. Some shouted one thing and some another. Since he couldn't find out the truth in all the uproar and confusion, he ordered that Paul be taken to the fortress. As Paul reached the stairs, the mob grew so violent the soldiers had to lift him to their shoulders to protect him. And the crowd followed behind, shouting, "Kill him, kill him!"

Paul Speaks to the Crowd

As Paul was about to be taken inside, he said to the commander, "May I have a word with you?"

"Do you know Greek?" the commander asked, surprised. "Aren't you the Egyptian who led a rebellion some time ago and took 4,000 members of the Assassins out into the desert?"

"No," Paul replied, "I am a Jew and a citizen of Tarsus in Cilicia, which is an important city. Please, let me talk to these people." The commander agreed, so Paul stood on the stairs and motioned to the people to be quiet. Soon a deep silence enveloped the crowd, and he addressed them in their own language, Aramaic.

CHAPTER
TWENTY-TWO

"Brothers and esteemed fathers," Paul said, "listen to me as I offer my defense." When they heard him speaking in their own language, the silence was even greater.

Then Paul said, "I am a Jew, born in Tarsus, a city in Cilicia, and I was brought up and educated here in Jerusalem under Gamaliel. As his student, I was carefully trained in our Jewish laws and customs. I became very zealous to honor God in everything I did, just like all of you today. And I persecuted the followers of the Way, hounding some to death, arresting both men and women and throwing them in prison. The high priest and the whole council of elders can testify that this is so. For I received letters from them to our Jewish brothers in Damascus, authorizing me to bring the followers of the Way from there to Jerusalem, in chains, to be punished.

"As I was on the road, approaching Damascus about noon, a very bright light from heaven suddenly shone down around me. I fell to the ground and heard a voice saying to me, 'Saul, Saul, why are you persecuting me?'

"'Who are you, lord?' I asked.

"And the voice replied, 'I am Jesus the Nazarene, the one you are persecuting.' The people with me saw the light but didn't understand the voice speaking to me.

"I asked, 'What should I do, Lord?'

"And the Lord told me, 'Get up and go into Damascus, and there you will be told everything you are to do.'

"I was blinded by the intense light and had to be led by the hand to Damascus by my companions. A man named Ananias lived there. He was a godly man, deeply devoted to the law, and well regarded by all the Jews of Damascus. He came and stood beside me and said, 'Brother Saul, regain your sight.' And that very moment I could see him!

"Then he told me, 'The God of our ancestors has chosen you to know his will and to see the Righteous One and hear him speak. For you are to be his witness, telling everyone what you have seen and heard. What are you waiting for? Get up and be baptized. Have your sins washed away by calling on the name of the Lord.'

"After I returned to Jerusalem, I was praying in the Temple and fell into a trance. I saw a vision of Jesus saying to me, 'Hurry! Leave Jerusalem, for the people here won't accept your testimony about me.'

"'But Lord,' I argued, 'they certainly know that in every synagogue I imprisoned and beat those who believed in you. And I was in complete agreement when your witness Stephen was killed. I stood by and kept the coats they took off when they stoned him.'

"But the Lord said to me, 'Go, for I will send you far away to the Gentiles!'"

The crowd listened until Paul said that word. Then they all began to shout, "Away with such a fellow! He isn't fit to live!" They yelled, threw off their coats, and tossed handfuls of dust into the air.

Paul Reveals His Roman Citizenship

The commander brought Paul inside and ordered him lashed with whips to make him confess his crime. He wanted to find out why the crowd had become so furious. When they tied Paul down to lash him, Paul said to the officer standing there, "Is it legal for you to whip a Roman citizen who hasn't even been tried?"

When the officer heard this, he went to the commander and asked, "What are you doing? This man is a Roman citizen!"

So the commander went over and asked Paul, "Tell me, are you a Roman citizen?"

"Yes, I certainly am," Paul replied.

"I am, too," the commander muttered, "and it cost me plenty!"

Paul answered, "But I am a citizen by birth!"

The soldiers who were about to interrogate Paul quickly withdrew when they heard he was a Roman citizen, and the commander was frightened because he had ordered him bound and whipped.

PAUL BEFORE THE HIGH COUNCIL

The next day the commander ordered the leading priests into session with the Jewish high council. He wanted to find out what the trouble was all about, so he released Paul to have him stand before them.

CHAPTER
TWENTY-THREE

Gazing intently at the high council, Paul began: "Brothers, I have always lived before God with a clear conscience!"

Instantly Ananias the high priest commanded those close to Paul to slap him on the mouth. But Paul said to him, "God will slap you, you corrupt hypocrite! What kind of judge are you to break the law yourself by ordering me struck like that?"

Those standing near Paul said to him, "Do you dare to insult God's high priest?"

"I'm sorry, brothers. I didn't realize he was the high priest," Paul replied, "for the Scriptures say, 'You must not speak evil of any of your rulers.'"

Paul realized that some members of the high council were Sadducees and some were Pharisees, so he shouted, "Brothers, I am a Pharisee, as were my ancestors! And I am on trial because my hope is in the resurrection of the dead!"

This divided the council—the Pharisees against the Sadducees—for the Sadducees say there is no resurrection or angels or spirits, but the Pharisees believe in all of these. So there was a great uproar. Some of the teachers of religious law who were Pharisees jumped up and began to argue forcefully. "We see nothing wrong with him," they shouted. "Perhaps a spirit or an angel spoke to him." As the conflict grew more violent, the commander was afraid they would tear Paul apart. So he ordered his soldiers to go and rescue him by force and take him back to the fortress.

That night the Lord appeared to Paul and said, "Be encouraged, Paul. Just as you have been a witness to me here in Jerusalem, you must preach the Good News in Rome as well."

The Plan to Kill Paul

The next morning a group of Jews got together and bound themselves with an oath not to eat or drink until they had killed Paul. There were more than forty of them in the conspiracy. They went to the leading priests and elders and told them, "We have bound ourselves with an oath to eat nothing until we have killed Paul. So you and the high council should ask the commander to bring Paul back to the council again. Pretend you want to examine his case more fully. We will kill him on the way."

But Paul's nephew—his sister's son—heard of their plan and went to the fortress and told Paul. Paul called for one of the Roman officers and said,

"Take this young man to the commander. He has something important to tell him."

So the officer did, explaining, "Paul, the prisoner, called me over and asked me to bring this young man to you because he has something to tell you."

The commander took his hand, led him aside, and asked, "What is it you want to tell me?"

Paul's nephew told him, "Some Jews are going to ask you to bring Paul before the high council tomorrow, pretending they want to get some more information. But don't do it! There are more than forty men hiding along the way ready to ambush him. They have vowed not to eat or drink anything until they have killed him. They are ready now, just waiting for your consent."

"Don't let anyone know you told me this," the commander warned the young man.

PAUL IS SENT TO CAESAREA

Then the commander called two of his officers and ordered, "Get 200 soldiers ready to leave for Caesarea at nine o'clock tonight. Also take 200 spearmen and 70 mounted troops. Provide horses for Paul to ride, and get him safely to Governor Felix." Then he wrote this letter to the governor:

"From Claudius Lysias, to his Excellency, Governor Felix: Greetings!

"This man was seized by some Jews, and they were about to kill him when I

arrived with the troops. When I learned
that he was a Roman citizen, I removed
him to safety. Then I took him to their
high council to try to learn the basis
of the accusations against him. I soon
discovered the charge was something
regarding their religious law—certainly
nothing worthy of imprisonment or death.
But when I was informed of a plot to kill
him, I immediately sent him on to you.
I have told his accusers to bring their
charges before you."

So that night, as ordered, the soldiers took Paul as
far as Antipatris. They returned to the fortress the
next morning, while the mounted troops took him
on to Caesarea. When they arrived in Caesarea, they
presented Paul and the letter to Governor Felix. He
read it and then asked Paul what province he was
from. "Cilicia," Paul answered.

"I will hear your case myself when your accusers arrive," the governor told him. Then the governor ordered him kept in the prison at Herod's
headquarters.

CHAPTER
TWENTY-FOUR

Paul Appears before Felix

Five days later Ananias, the high priest, arrived with some of the Jewish elders and the lawyer Tertullus, to present their case against Paul to the governor. When Paul was called in, Tertullus presented the charges against Paul in the following address to the governor:

"You have provided a long period of peace for us Jews and with foresight have enacted reforms for us. For all of this, Your Excellency, we are very grateful to you. But I don't want to bore you, so please give me your attention for only a moment. We have found this man to be a troublemaker who is constantly stirring up riots among the Jews all over the world. He is a ringleader of the cult known as the Nazarenes. Furthermore, he was trying to desecrate the Temple when we arrested him. You can find out the truth of our accusations by examining him your-self." Then the other Jews chimed in, declaring that everything Tertullus said was true.

The governor then motioned for Paul to speak. Paul said, "I know, sir, that you have been a judge of Jewish affairs for many years, so I gladly present my defense before you. You can quickly discover that I arrived in Jerusalem no more than twelve days ago to worship at the Temple. My accusers never found me arguing with anyone in the Temple, nor stirring up a riot in any synagogue or on the streets of the city. These men cannot prove the things they accuse me of doing.

"But I admit that I follow the Way, which they call a cult. I worship the God of our ancestors, and I firmly believe the Jewish law and everything written in the prophets. I have the same hope in God that these men have, that he will raise both the righteous and the unrighteous. Because of this, I always try to maintain a clear conscience before God and all people.

"After several years away, I returned to Jerusalem with money to aid my people and to offer sacrifices to God. My accusers saw me in the Temple as I was completing a purification ceremony. There was no crowd around me and no rioting. But some Jews from the province of Asia were there—and they ought to be here to bring charges if they have anything against me! Ask these men here what crime the Jewish high council found me guilty of, except for the one time I shouted out, 'I am on trial before you today because I believe in the resurrection of the dead!'"

At that point Felix, who was quite familiar with the Way, adjourned the hearing and said, "Wait until Lysias, the garrison commander, arrives. Then I will decide the case." He ordered an officer to keep Paul in custody but to give him some freedom and allow his friends to visit him and take care of his needs.

A few days later Felix came back with his wife, Drusilla, who was Jewish. Sending for Paul, they listened as he told them about faith in Christ Jesus. As he reasoned with them about righteousness and self-control and the coming day of judgment, Felix became frightened. "Go away for now," he replied. "When it is more convenient, I'll call for you again." He also hoped that Paul would bribe him, so he sent for him quite often and talked with him.

After two years went by in this way, Felix was succeeded by Porcius Festus. And because Felix wanted to gain favor with the Jewish people, he left Paul in prison.

TWENTY-FIVE

Paul Appears before Festus

Three days after Festus arrived in Caesarea to take over his new responsibilities, he left for Jerusalem, where the leading priests and other Jewish leaders met with him and made their accusations against Paul. They asked Festus as a favor to transfer Paul to Jerusalem (planning to ambush and kill him on the way). But Festus replied that Paul was at Caesarea and he himself would be returning there soon. So he said, "Those of you in authority can return with me. If Paul has done anything wrong, you can make your accusations."

About eight or ten days later Festus returned to Caesarea, and on the following day he took his seat in court and ordered that Paul be brought in. When Paul arrived, the Jewish leaders from Jerusalem gathered around and made many serious accusations they couldn't prove.

Paul denied the charges. "I am not guilty of any crime against the Jewish laws or the Temple or the Roman government," he said.

Then Festus, wanting to please the Jews, asked him, "Are you willing to go to Jerusalem and stand trial before me there?"

But Paul replied, "No! This is the official Roman court, so I ought to be tried right here. You know very well I am not guilty of harming the Jews. If I have done something worthy of death, I don't refuse to die. But if I am innocent, no one has a right to turn me over to these men to kill me. I appeal to Caesar!"

Festus conferred with his advisers and then replied, "Very well! You have appealed to Caesar, and to Caesar you will go!"

A few days later King Agrippa arrived with his sister, Bernice, to pay their respects to Festus. During their stay of several days, Festus discussed Paul's case with the king. "There is a prisoner here," he told him, "whose case was left for me by Felix. When I was in Jerusalem, the leading priests and Jewish elders pressed charges against him and asked me to condemn him. I pointed out to them that Roman law does not convict people without a trial. They must be given an opportunity to confront their accusers and defend themselves.

"When his accusers came here for the trial, I didn't delay. I called the case the very next day and ordered Paul brought in. But the accusations made

HEROD AGRIPPA II

Like great-grandfather, like grandfather, like father, like son—this tells the story of Herod Agrippa II. He inherited the character flaws of generations of powerful men. Each generation had a confrontation with God but failed to realize the importance of the moment.

Like so many before and after, Agrippa II heard about the Kingdom of God but decided it wasn't worth responding to personally. He left himself without excuse.

What has been your response to the gospel? It may seem like too great a price to give God control of your life, but the price is minimal compared to living apart from him for eternity because you have chosen not to be his child.

+ **STRENGTHS AND ACCOMPLISHMENTS:** Last ruler of the Herod dynasty, which ruled parts of Palestine from 40 B.C. to A.D. 100

Continued his father's success in mediating between Rome and Palestine

Maintained the family tradition of building and improving cities

+ **WEAKNESSES AND MISTAKES:** Was not convinced by the gospel and consciously rejected it

Carried on an incestuous relationship with his sister Bernice

+ **LESSONS FROM HIS LIFE:** Families pass on both positive and negative influences to children

There are no guarantees of multiple opportunities to respond to God

+ **VITAL STATISTICS:** Occupation: Ruler of northern and eastern Palestine

Relatives: Great-grandfather: Herod the Great. Father: Herod Agrippa I. Great-uncle: Herod Antipas. Sisters: Bernice, Mariamne, Drusilla.

against him weren't any of the crimes I expected. Instead, it was something about their religion and a dead man named Jesus, who Paul insists is alive. I was at a loss to know how to investigate these things, so I asked him whether he would be willing to stand trial on these charges in Jerusalem. But Paul appealed to have his case decided by the emperor. So I ordered that he be held in custody until I could arrange to send him to Caesar."

"I'd like to hear the man myself," Agrippa said.

And Festus replied, "You will—tomorrow!"

PAUL SPEAKS TO AGRIPPA

So the next day Agrippa and Bernice arrived at the auditorium with great pomp, accompanied by military officers and prominent men of the city. Festus ordered that Paul be brought in. Then Festus said, "King Agrippa and all who are here, this is the man whose death is demanded by all the Jews, both here and in Jerusalem. But in my opinion he has done nothing deserving death. However, since he appealed his case to the emperor, I have decided to send him to Rome.

"But what shall I write the emperor? For there is no clear charge against him. So I have brought him before all of you, and especially you, King Agrippa, so that after we examine him, I might have something to write. For it makes no sense to send a prisoner to the emperor without specifying the charges against him!"

CHAPTER
TWENTY-SIX

Then Agrippa said to Paul, "You may speak in your defense."

So Paul, gesturing with his hand, started his defense: "I am fortunate, King Agrippa, that you are the one hearing my defense today against all these accusations made by the Jewish leaders, for I know you are an expert on all Jewish customs and controversies. Now please listen to me patiently!

"As the Jewish leaders are well aware, I was given a thorough Jewish training from my earliest childhood among my own people and in Jerusalem. If they would admit it, they know that I have been a member of the Pharisees, the strictest sect of our religion. Now I am on trial because of my hope in the fulfillment of God's promise made to our ancestors. In fact, that is why the twelve tribes of Israel zealously worship God night and day, and they share the same hope I have. Yet, Your Majesty, they accuse me for having this hope! Why does it seem incredible to any of you that God can raise the dead?

"I used to believe that I ought to do everything I could to oppose the very name of Jesus the Nazarene. Indeed, I did just that in Jerusalem. Authorized by the leading priests, I caused many believers there to be sent to prison. And I cast my vote against them when they were condemned to death. Many times I had them punished in the synagogues to get them to curse Jesus. I was so violently opposed to them that I even chased them down in foreign cities.

"One day I was on such a mission to Damascus, armed with the authority and commission of the leading priests. About noon, Your Majesty, as I was on the road, a light from heaven brighter than the sun shone down on me and my companions. We all fell down, and I heard a voice saying to me in Aramaic, 'Saul, Saul, why are you persecuting me? It is useless for you to fight against my will.'

"'Who are you, lord?' I asked.

"And the Lord replied, 'I am Jesus, the one you are persecuting. Now get to your feet! For I have appeared to you to appoint you as my servant and witness. Tell people that you have seen me, and tell them what I will show you in the future. And I will rescue you from both your own people and the Gentiles. Yes, I am sending you to the Gentiles to open their eyes, so they may turn from darkness to light and from the power of Satan to God. Then they will receive forgiveness for their sins and be given a place among God's people, who are set apart by faith in me.'

"And so, King Agrippa, I obeyed that vision from

heaven. I preached first to those in Damascus, then in Jerusalem and throughout all Judea, and also to the Gentiles, that all must repent of their sins and turn to God—and prove they have changed by the good things they do. Some Jews arrested me in the Temple for preaching this, and they tried to kill me. But God has protected me right up to this present time so I can testify to everyone, from the least to the greatest. I teach nothing except what the prophets and Moses said would happen—that the Messiah would suffer and be the first to rise from the dead, and in this way announce God's light to Jews and Gentiles alike."

Suddenly, Festus shouted, "Paul, you are insane. Too much study has made you crazy!"

But Paul replied, "I am not insane, Most Excellent Festus. What I am saying is the sober truth. And King Agrippa knows about these things. I speak boldly, for I am sure these events are all familiar to him, for they were not done in a corner! King Agrippa, do you believe the prophets? I know you do—"

Agrippa interrupted him. "Do you think you can persuade me to become a Christian so quickly?"

Paul replied, "Whether quickly or not, I pray to God that both you and everyone here in this audience might become the same as I am, except for these chains."

Then the king, the governor, Bernice, and all the others stood and left. As they went out, they talked it over and agreed, "This man hasn't done anything to deserve death or imprisonment."

And Agrippa said to Festus, "He could have been set free if he hadn't appealed to Caesar."

TWENTY-SEVEN

Paul Sails for Rome

When the time came, we set sail for Italy. Paul and several other prisoners were placed in the custody of a Roman officer named Julius, a captain of the Imperial Regiment. Aristarchus, a Macedonian from Thessalonica, was also with us. We left on a ship whose home port was Adramyttium on the northwest coast of the province of Asia; it was scheduled to make several stops at ports along the coast of the province.

The next day when we docked at Sidon, Julius was very kind to Paul and let him go ashore to visit with friends so they could provide for his needs. Putting out to sea from there, we encountered strong headwinds that made it difficult to keep the ship on course, so we sailed north of Cyprus between the island and the mainland. Keeping to the open sea, we passed along the coast of Cilicia and Pamphylia, landing at Myra, in the province of Lycia. There the commanding officer found an Egyptian ship from Alexandria that was bound for Italy, and he put us on board.

We had several days of slow sailing, and after great difficulty we finally neared Cnidus. But the wind was against us, so we sailed across to Crete and along the sheltered coast of the island, past the cape of Salmone. We struggled along the coast with great difficulty and finally arrived at Fair Havens, near the town of Lasea. We had lost a lot of time. The weather was becoming dangerous for sea travel because it was so late in the fall, and Paul spoke to the ship's officers about it.

"Men," he said, "I believe there is trouble ahead if we go on—shipwreck, loss of cargo, and danger to our lives as well." But the officer in charge of the prisoners listened more to the ship's captain and the owner than to Paul. And since Fair Havens was an exposed harbor—a poor place to spend the winter—most of the crew wanted to go on to Phoenix, farther up the coast of Crete, and spend the winter there. Phoenix was a good harbor with only a southwest and northwest exposure.

THE STORM AT SEA

When a light wind began blowing from the south, the sailors thought they could make it. So they pulled up anchor and sailed close to the shore of Crete. But the weather changed abruptly, and a wind of typhoon strength (called a "northeaster") burst across the island and blew us out to sea. The sailors couldn't turn the ship into the wind, so they gave up and let it run before the gale.

We sailed along the sheltered side of a small island named Cauda, where with great difficulty we hoisted aboard the lifeboat being towed behind us. Then the sailors bound ropes around the hull of the ship to strengthen it. They were afraid of being driven across to the sandbars of Syrtis off the African coast, so they lowered the sea anchor to slow the ship and were driven before the wind.

The next day, as gale-force winds continued to batter the ship, the crew began throwing the cargo overboard. The following day they even took some of the ship's gear and threw it overboard. The terrible storm raged for many days, blotting out the sun and the stars, until at last all hope was gone.

No one had eaten for a long time. Finally, Paul called the crew together and said, "Men, you should have listened to me in the first place and not left Crete. You would have avoided all this damage and loss. But take courage! None of you will lose your lives, even though the ship will go down. For last night an angel of the God to whom I belong and whom I serve stood beside me, and he said, 'Don't be afraid, Paul, for you will surely stand trial before Caesar! What's more, God in his goodness has granted safety to everyone sailing with you.' So take courage! For I believe God. It will be just as he said. But we will be shipwrecked on an island."

The Shipwreck

About midnight on the fourteenth night of the storm, as we were being driven across the Sea of Adria, the sailors sensed land was near. They dropped a weighted line and found that the water was 120 feet deep. But a little later they measured again and found it was only 90 feet deep. At this rate they were afraid we would soon be driven against the rocks along the shore, so they threw out four anchors from the back of the ship and prayed for daylight.

Then the sailors tried to abandon the ship; they lowered the lifeboat as though they were going to put out anchors from the front of the ship. But Paul said to the commanding officer and the soldiers, "You will all die unless the sailors stay aboard." So the soldiers cut the ropes to the lifeboat and let it drift away.

Just as day was dawning, Paul urged everyone to eat. "You have been so worried that you haven't touched food for two weeks," he said. "Please eat something now for your own good. For not a hair of your heads will perish." Then he took some bread, gave thanks to God before them all, and broke off a piece and ate it. Then everyone was encouraged and began to eat—all 276 of us who were on board. After eating, the crew lightened the ship further by throwing the cargo of wheat overboard.

When morning dawned, they didn't recognize the coastline, but they saw a bay with a beach and wondered if they could get to shore by running the ship aground. So they cut off the anchors and left them in the sea. Then they lowered the rudders, raised the foresail, and headed toward shore. But they hit a shoal and ran the ship aground too soon. The bow of the ship stuck fast, while the stern was repeatedly smashed by the force of the waves and began to break apart.

The soldiers wanted to kill the prisoners to make sure they didn't swim ashore and escape. But the commanding officer wanted to spare Paul, so he didn't let them carry out their plan. Then he ordered all who could swim to jump overboard first and make for land. The others held on to planks or debris from the broken ship. So everyone escaped safely to shore.

CHAPTER

TWENTY-EIGHT

PAUL ON THE ISLAND OF MALTA

Once we were safe on shore, we learned that we were on the island of Malta. The people of the island were very kind to us. It was cold and rainy, so they built a fire on the shore to welcome us.

As Paul gathered an armful of sticks and was laying them on the fire, a poisonous snake, driven out by the heat, bit him on the hand. The people of the island saw it hanging from his hand and said to each other, "A murderer, no doubt! Though he escaped the sea, justice will not permit him to live." But Paul shook off the snake into the fire and was unharmed. The people waited for him to swell up or suddenly drop dead. But when they had waited a long time and saw that he wasn't harmed, they changed their minds and decided he was a god.

Near the shore where we landed was an estate belonging to Publius, the chief official of the island. He welcomed us and treated us kindly for three days. As it happened, Publius's father was ill with fever and dysentery. Paul went in and prayed for him, and laying his hands on him, he healed him. Then all the other sick people on the island came and were healed. As a result we were showered with honors, and when the time came to sail, people supplied us with everything we would need for the trip.

PAUL ARRIVES AT ROME

It was three months after the shipwreck that we set sail on another ship that had wintered at the island—an Alexandrian ship with the twin gods as its figurehead. Our first stop was Syracuse, where we stayed three days. From there we sailed across to Rhegium. A day later a south wind began blowing, so the following day we sailed up the coast to Puteoli. There we found some believers, who invited us to spend a week with them. And so we came to Rome.

The brothers and sisters in Rome had heard we were coming, and they came to meet us at the Forum on the Appian Way. Others joined us at The Three Taverns. When Paul saw them, he was encouraged and thanked God.

When we arrived in Rome, Paul was permitted to have his own private lodging, though he was guarded by a soldier.

Paul Preaches at Rome under Guard

Three days after Paul's arrival, he called together the local Jewish leaders. He said to them, "Brothers, I was arrested in Jerusalem and handed over to the Roman government, even though I had done nothing against our people or the customs of our ancestors. The Romans tried me and wanted to release me, because they found no cause for the death sentence. But when the Jewish leaders protested the decision, I felt it necessary to appeal to Caesar, even though I had no desire to press charges against my own people. I asked you to come here today so we could get acquainted and so I could explain to you that I am bound with this chain because I believe that the hope of Israel—the Messiah—has already come."

They replied, "We have had no letters from Judea or reports against you from anyone who has come here. But we want to hear what you believe, for the only thing we know about this movement is that it is denounced everywhere."

So a time was set, and on that day a large number of people came to Paul's lodging. He explained and testified about the Kingdom of God and tried to persuade them about Jesus from the Scriptures. Using the law of Moses and the books of the prophets, he spoke to them from morning until evening. Some were persuaded by the things he said, but others did not believe. And after they had argued back and forth among themselves, they left with this final word from Paul: "The Holy Spirit was right when he said to your ancestors through Isaiah the prophet,

'Go and say to this people:
When you hear what I say,
*   you will not understand.*
When you see what I do,
*   you will not comprehend.*
For the hearts of these people are hardened,
*   and their ears cannot hear,*
*   and they have closed their eyes—*
so their eyes cannot see,
*   and their ears cannot hear,*
*   and their hearts cannot understand,*
and they cannot turn to me
*   and let me heal them.'*

So I want you to know that this salvation from God has also been offered to the Gentiles, and they will accept it."

For the next two years, Paul lived in Rome at his own expense. He welcomed all who visited him, boldly proclaiming the Kingdom of God and teaching about the Lord Jesus Christ. And no one tried to stop him.

EPILOGUE

EPILOGUE

THE CALL OF JESUS

"Look, I am coming soon, bringing
my reward with me to repay all people
according to their deeds. I am the Alpha
and the Omega, the First and the Last, the
Beginning and the End."

Blessed are those who wash their robes. They
will be permitted to enter through the gates of the
city and eat the fruit from the tree of life. Outside
the city are the dogs—the sorcerers, the sexually
immoral, the murderers, the idol worshipers, and
all who love to live a lie.

"I, Jesus, have sent my angel to give you
this message for the churches. I am both
the source of David and the heir to his
throne. I am the bright morning star."

The Spirit and the bride say, "Come." Let anyone who hears this say, "Come." Let anyone who is thirsty come. Let anyone who desires drink freely from the water of life.

THE HISTORY OF THE CHURCH

Think of all the things that have turned the world upside down: controlled fire, the invention of the wheel, the written alphabet, the printing press, the automobile—and more recently, the Internet and the digital age. And there will be more revolutions to come.

But there was something that happened in the first century A.D. that overshadows all other changes in history—something that completely turned the world upside down. That's precisely how some religious leaders described the followers of Jesus Christ in Thessalonica: "these who have turned the world upside down" (Acts 17:6, NKJV). For one thing, the gospel was upsetting established religious traditions, and on top of that, lots of people were believing it. This wasn't just a localized reaction, either: there were converts throughout the Mediterranean world (Acts 5:14; 6:1, 7; 9:31, 35, 42; 11:21, 24; 14:21; 16:14; 17:4, 12; 28:30-31).

No church in history has accomplished more than the first-century church, which began in Jerusalem. Within months of its inception, tens of thousands of people were added to the original 120 members. Within a few years, the church spread from Jerusalem to Judea, Samaria, and Galilee, and into Asia Minor. By the end of the apostolic era, the church had grown as far west as Rome—and possibly Spain (Romans 15:24, 28).

But the impact wasn't just numerical. Historian Rodney Stark paints a picture of what the early church looked like:

> Christianity revitalized life in Greco-Roman
> cities by providing new norms and new kinds
> of social relationships able to cope with many
> urgent urban problems. To cities filled with the
> homeless and impoverished, Christianity offered
> charity as well as hope. To cities filled with new-
> comers and strangers, Christianity offered an
> immediate basis for attachments. To cities filled

with orphans and widows, Christianity provided
a new and expanded sense of family. To cities
torn by violent ethnic strife, Christianity offered
a new basis for social solidarity. . . . And to cities
faced with epidemics, fire, and earthquakes,
Christianity offered effective nursing services. . . .
For what they brought was not simply an urban
movement, but a new culture capable of making
life in Greco-Roman cities more tolerable.[1]

When we consider the resources the new church had
to work with (almost no money), the training (none, except
the teaching the twelve apostles received from Jesus),
the task facing them (reaching the world with the gospel),
and the opposition (the powerful religious and political
leaders of the day), what the early church achieved is a
phenomenon that has never been equaled.

So why did the early church catch like wildfire in
the Roman world? What accounts for their success?
Ultimately, the cause of the church's effectiveness in
spreading the gospel was the Holy Spirit. But there were
also four characteristics of the early church that enabled
the believers to make such an extraordinary impact on
their world.

CONVICTION

Jesus didn't just give his disciples good ideas. He gave
them his life. Because the disciples were witnesses to
the resurrection of Jesus Christ, they were convinced that
everything else he said was true as well. It was this knowledge that propelled the early church into the world with
the assurance, knowledge, and confidence they needed
to preach the message of Christ.

COMMISSION

The apostles didn't sit around wringing their hands, trying
to figure out what to do after Jesus returned to heaven.
They had marching orders from him—the great commission—that gave them a track to run on. The commission
of Christ to the disciples—take the gospel to the world—
dominated their lives. In our multifaceted churches, with

our many programs and committees, it's good for us to be reminded of the disciples' single-minded goal.

COMMITMENT
The early church was committed to being faithful to one thing: being witnesses for what they had seen and heard (Acts 4:19-20). There is no record in church history of any of the apostles ever wavering from their goal. They remained committed to Jesus' commission until their deaths—even to the point of martyrdom.

CONFIDENCE
The apostles weren't arrogant, but they were confident. Even the crowds in Jerusalem noticed their boldness. They concluded that the apostles "had been with Jesus" (Acts 4:13). After spending time with Jesus, the apostles possessed a newfound confidence and conviction that allowed them to overcome the persecution all around them.

THE CHURCH'S IMPACT ON THE WORLD
Since the days of the first-century church, Christianity has continued to grow and dramatically change the world. Today it remains the world's largest spiritual movement, followed by Islam and Hinduism. In recent years, the most remarkable change in religious demographics has been the shift in the "center" of Christendom. While Christianity in North America and Europe is either declining or static, the gospel is exploding in Asia, Africa, and Latin America. In some countries in these regions, Christianity is growing at an even faster rate than the population.[2]

Over the years, Christianity has been responsible for developments in medicine, science, education, government, law, literacy, charity, art, and other human endeavors. Whenever a tragedy or natural disaster occurs, it is Christians, more than any other group, who respond with the love, compassion, and servanthood of Christ. His compassion for the poor, the weak, the downtrodden, and the needy continues to motivate his followers to serve just as he did.

The Christian church has been commissioned to do even greater works than Jesus did (John 14:12). This doesn't mean greater in quality, but greater in quantity. To accomplish these good works, Christ sent the Holy Spirit to indwell his followers, empowering them to spread out across the globe and to be his hands and heart in the world. The church will continue to grow and show the world the love of Christ as Christians are faithful in fulfilling Jesus' call to go and make disciples of all nations (Matthew 28:19-20).

THE SECOND COMING OF JESUS

We live in a day of big world events. Even small events can seem huge with the way word seems to spread in milliseconds around the globe. But there is an event coming "soon" that will dwarf everything else that has happened in human history: the second coming of Jesus Christ.

Jesus Christ came the first time to deal with humankind's sin problem, making eternal life possible. When he comes the second time, he will make eternal life permanent. He will balance the scales of justice and set everything right: "Look, I am coming soon, bringing my reward with me to repay all people according to their deeds" (Revelation 22:12). Under Christ's rule, the world will enjoy a thousand years of righteousness (Revelation 20:1-6), Satan will be judged and consigned to eternal doom (Revelation 20:7-10), and God will judge all those whose names are not found in the Book of Life (Revelation 20:11-15).

For most people, the one burning question that comes to mind regarding the Second Coming is "When?" Jesus said there's only one who knows the answer to that question:

> No one knows the day or hour when these things will happen, not even the angels in heaven or the Son himself. Only the Father knows.
>
> MATTHEW 24:36

> The Father alone has the authority to set those dates and times, and they are not for you to know.
>
> ACTS 1:7

Instead of speculating about when Christ would return, Jesus told his apostles and followers that they

should focus on the commission he had given them—
to go into the world in the power of the Holy Spirit to
make disciples (Acts 1:8). Although they weren't given
specific information, there is every indication the apostles
thought his return would be soon. This was reflected in
their writing:

- "Take courage, for the coming of the Lord is near"
  (James 5:8).
- "The night is almost gone; the day of salvation will
  soon be here" (Romans 13:12).
- "We who are still living when the Lord returns . . ."
  (1 Thessalonians 4:15).
- "Dear children, the last hour is here" (1 John 2:18).
- "We are eagerly waiting for [Christ] to return as
  our Savior" (Philippians 3:20).
- "The God of peace will soon crush Satan under
  your feet" (Romans 16:20).

Those words (and many more like them) were written in the first century. Near the end of the first century,
Jesus said to the apostle John, "Look, I am coming soon!"
(Revelation 22:7, 12). But the way we interpret "soon"—as
a function of time—is obviously not what Jesus and the
apostles meant, because it has been nearly two thousand
years since those words were recorded. So what does
"soon" mean?

It is clear from Scripture that God doesn't mark time
in the same way that we do (2 Peter 3:8). God seems to
delineate time according to events, not days or years. So
when the New Testament writers said "soon," they were
referring to the next event on God's prophetic calendar—
the inauguration of the end of the age. The end of the age
we're currently living in will be marked by the Rapture
of the church (1 Thessalonians 4:13-18), followed by
Christ's second coming. That was true at the end of the
first century, and it is true today. Prophetically speaking,
"soon" means the same thing today as it did then: Jesus
could return for his church at any moment.

The disciples once asked Jesus, "What sign will signal
your return and the end of the world?" (Matthew 24:3).

Jesus gave them many signs to look for, including wars, famines, earthquakes, persecution, and false prophets (Matthew 24:4-16). Then he gave the final sign of his return: "At last, the sign that the Son of Man is coming will appear in the heavens. . . . And they will see the Son of Man coming on the clouds of heaven with power and great glory" (Matthew 24:30).

Jesus rebuked the religious leaders of his day for not knowing "how to interpret the signs of the times" (Matthew 16:3). Specifically, his rebuke was for their failure to recognize him, the Messiah, in their midst. Today, we should be careful that we are not guilty of the same charge. We should strive to be like the two hundred leaders of the Old Testament tribe of Issachar who were known for their discernment—men who "understood the signs of the times" (1 Chronicles 12:32).

When the apostle John heard Jesus say, "Look, I am coming soon" (Revelation 22:12), he wrote, "Let anyone who hears this say, 'Come.' Let anyone who is thirsty come. Let anyone who desires drink freely from the water of life" (Revelation 22:17).

The question to ask is not "When will Jesus return?" The question is "Am I ready for his return, regardless of when it is?"

At the end of this age, when Jesus returns with the blast of a trumpet, may we all be ready.

A CALL TO ACTION

A CALL
TO ACTION

SOMETIMES CHRISTIANS ARE accused of working toward contradictory ends. "You say the world is on a downward cycle—that things are going to get worse before they get better," the critics say. "Yet you're trying to make the world better by evangelizing and doing good works. Why don't you just sit back and let things run their course?" We are accused of polishing the brass and rearranging the deck chairs on a sinking ship—efforts that will eventually prove fruitless.

Throughout history, some have held that the church will transform the world into the Kingdom of Heaven on earth before Christ returns. They claim that Christ won't return until the church has brought peace on earth and goodwill toward men, after which he will return and assume his rightful role as King. But after centuries marked by worldwide wars and a series of other moral and cultural failings, it's hard to keep the wind in those theological sails. Humans have not succeeded in fully establishing the Kingdom of God "on earth as it is in heaven"— and we never will. The Bible is clear that Christ will come at a time when humankind is at its worst. Only then will he make all things right.

So what are we to do until then? We are to obediently fulfill Christ's final command to his apostles— to "go and make disciples of all the nations. . . . Teach these new disciples to obey all the commands I have given you. And be sure of this: I am with you always, even *to the end of the age*" (Matthew 28:19-20, emphasis added). It is clear from that last phrase that Jesus never intended for us to stop making disciples until he returned. Why would he have promised to be with us to the end of the age if he didn't mean for us to continue fulfilling his commission right up until the end—that is, right up until his return?

After all, that's what the book of Acts is all about. Luke wrote an entire book about what Matthew describes in these two verses—about how Christ works through his followers by the power of the Holy Spirit to disciple all nations.

The main action of the book of Acts ends around A.D. 62, with the apostle Paul's last missionary journey wrapping up around A.D. 67 (2 Timothy 4). That's why some have labeled the ensuing nineteen-plus centuries "Acts 29"—what the Spirit has been doing in the world through the church since Acts ended with chapter 28.

This brings us to a question we must ask ourselves: "Are we carrying out Christ's commission to make disciples of the nations?" And an even more important question: "Have we accepted the gospel of Christ personally?" The fact is, we can't give away to others what we don't possess ourselves.

Thankfully, the Bible shows us how we can possess eternal life. In just twenty-five words, this verse succinctly tells the story of God and his plan for this world: "For God so loved the world that He gave His only begotten Son, that whoever believes in Him should not perish but have everlasting life" (John 3:16, NKJV).

John 3:16 is the message I love to tell others about. It is arguably the greatest picture of God's love in the Bible and the greatest verse in the Bible. In fact, the greatness of this verse has been summarized with these words:

> God—the greatest lover
> so loved—the greatest love
> the world—the greatest number
> that He gave—the greatest gift
> His only begotten Son—the greatest Person
> that whoever—the greatest opportunity
> believes—the greatest simplicity
> in Him—the greatest attraction
> should not perish—the greatest promise
> but—the greatest difference
> have—the greatest certainty
> everlasting life—the greatest possession

Yes, the greatness of God's love has been demonstrated by the giving of the most expensive gift to the world. God looked around heaven for the most extravagant way he could demonstrate his love for lost human beings. Then he put his hand on the shoulder of Jesus and sent him—his only Son—into this world to pay the price for our sin and give us eternal life.

To this great truth, God only asks you to respond in faith. His love for you will prove useless if you don't believe in Christ. But eternal life—and a redeemed relationship with God—begins the moment you place your trust in Jesus. Jesus said, "I am the way, the truth, and the life. No one can come to the Father except through me" (John 14:6; see also John 17:3).

There are many significant decisions we must all make in life, but none is more important than how we respond to the salvation offered to us through Jesus Christ. Would you place your trust in him? If you do, you will begin to experience eternal life— life like the wonderful adventure you have just read about in the book of Acts!

APPENDIX 1

Maps

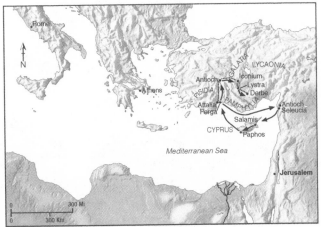

PAUL'S FIRST MISSIONARY JOURNEY (ACTS chapters 13–14)

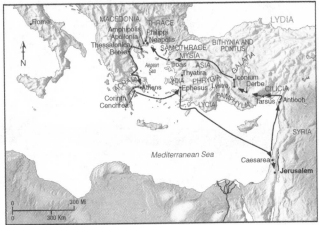

PAUL'S SECOND MISSIONARY JOURNEY (ACTS chapters15–18)

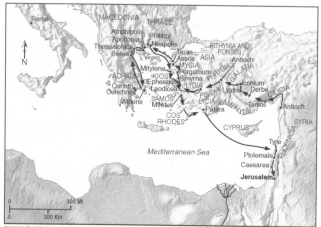

PAUL'S THIRD MISSIONARY JOURNEY (ACTS chapters 18–21)

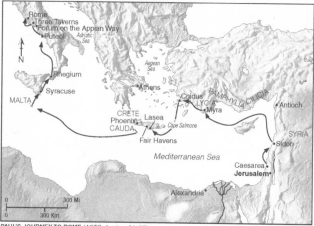

PAUL'S JOURNEY TO ROME (ACTS chapters 21–28)

APPENDIX 2

Favorite Verses

Jesus said, "Father, forgive them, for they don't know what they are doing."
PROLOGUE, page 5

Jesus replied, "I assure you, today you will be with me in paradise."
PROLOGUE, page 5

Jesus shouted, "Father, I entrust my spirit into your hands!"
PROLOGUE, page 5

Why are you looking among the dead for someone who is alive? He isn't here! He is risen from the dead!
PROLOGUE, page 8

[Jesus asked,] "Why are your hearts filled with doubt? Look at my hands. Look at my feet. You can see that it's really me."
PROLOGUE, page 10

You will receive power when the Holy
Spirit comes upon you. And you will be
my witnesses, telling people about me
everywhere—in Jerusalem, throughout
Judea, in Samaria, and to the ends of
the earth.

ACTS CHAPTER 1, page 20

God raised Jesus from the dead, and we are
all witnesses of this.

ACTS CHAPTER 2, page 27

All the believers devoted themselves to the
apostles' teaching, and to fellowship, and
to sharing in meals (including the Lord's
Supper), and to prayer.

ACTS CHAPTER 2, page 28

Each day the Lord added to their fellowship
those who were being saved.

ACTS CHAPTER 2, page 28

I don't have any silver or gold for you. But
I'll give you what I have. In the name of
Jesus Christ the Nazarene, get up and walk!

ACTS CHAPTER 3, page 29

The members of the council were amazed
when they saw the boldness of Peter and
John, for they could see that they were
ordinary men with no special training

in the Scriptures. They also recognized
them as men who had been with Jesus.

ACTS CHAPTER 4, page 33

The apostles were performing many
miraculous signs and wonders among the
people. . . . Crowds came from the villages
around Jerusalem, bringing their sick and
those possessed by evil spirits, and they
were all healed.

ACTS CHAPTER 5, page 37

If they are planning and doing these
things merely on their own, it will soon be
overthrown. But if it is from God, you will
not be able to overthrow them. You may
even find yourselves fighting against God!

ACTS CHAPTER 5, page 39

As they stoned him, Stephen prayed, "Lord
Jesus, receive my spirit." He fell to his
knees, shouting, "Lord, don't charge them
with this sin!"

ACTS CHAPTER 7, page 49

The Lord said, "Go, for Saul is my chosen
instrument to take my message to the
Gentiles and to kings, as well as to the
people of Israel."

ACTS CHAPTER 9, page 56

Peter replied, "I see very clearly that God shows no favoritism. In every nation he accepts those who fear him and do what is right."

ACTS CHAPTER 10, page 65

This is the message of Good News for the people of Israel—that there is peace with God through Jesus Christ, who is Lord of all.

ACTS CHAPTER 10, page 65

The word of God continued to spread, and there were many new believers.

ACTS CHAPTER 12, page 74

We are here to proclaim that through this man Jesus there is forgiveness for your sins. Everyone who believes in him is declared right with God—something the law of Moses could never do.

ACTS CHAPTER 13, page 79

He is the God who made the world and everything in it. Since he is Lord of heaven and earth, he doesn't live in man-made temples, and human hands can't serve his needs—for he has no needs. He himself gives life and breath to everything, and he satisfies every need. . . . For in him we live and move and exist.

ACTS CHAPTER 17, page 100–101

My life is worth nothing to me unless I use it for finishing the work assigned me by the Lord Jesus—the work of telling others the Good News about the wonderful grace of God.

ACTS CHAPTER 20, page 115

NOTES

INTRODUCTION
1. D. A. Carson, *How Long, O Lord?: Reflections on Suffering and Evil* (Grand Rapids, MI: Baker Academic, 2006), 201.
2. Charles Adamson Salmond, *Princetoniana: Charles & A. A. Hodge: With Class and Table Talk of Hodge the Younger* (New York: Scribner and Welford, 1888), 181.

THE LAST DAYS OF JESUS
1. John Stott, *The Contemporary Christian* (Downers Grove, IL: InterVarsity Press, 1992), 81.

THE CALL OF JESUS
1. Rodney Stark, *The Rise of Christianity: How the Obscure, Marginal Jesus Movement Became the Dominant Religious Force in the Western World in a Few Centuries* (New York: HarperOne, 1997), 161–62.
2. See Philip Jenkins, *The Next Christendom: The Coming of Global Christianity*, 3rd ed. (New York: Oxford University Press, 2011) and Miriam Adeney, *Kingdom without Borders: The Untold Story of Global Christianity* (Downers Grove, IL: InterVarsity Press, 2009).

ABOUT THE AUTHOR

Dr. David Jeremiah serves as senior pastor of Shadow Mountain Community Church in El Cajon, California. He is the founder and host of Turning Point, a ministry committed to providing Christians with sound Bible teaching relevant to today's changing times through radio, television, the Internet, live events, and resource materials and books. A bestselling author, Dr. Jeremiah has written more than forty books, including *Captured by Grace*, *Living with Confidence in a Chaotic World*, *What in the World Is Going On?*, *The Coming Economic Armageddon*, *God Loves You: He Always Has—He Always Will*, *What Are You Afraid Of?*, and *Agents of the Apocalypse*.

Dr. Jeremiah's commitment to teaching the complete Word of God continues to make him a sought-after speaker and writer. His passion for reaching the lost and encouraging believers in their faith is demonstrated through his faithful communication of biblical truths.

A dedicated family man, Dr. Jeremiah and his wife, Donna, have four grown children and twelve grandchildren.

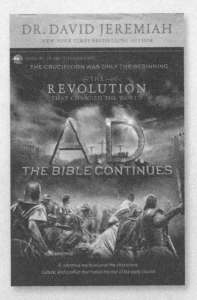